Disappearing In Glimpses

Geneva Phillips

MONGREL EMPIRE PRESS
NORMAN, OKLAHOMA, UNITED STATES OF AMERICA

2020

FIRST EDITION, 2020

Disappearing in Glimpses
© 2020 by Geneva Phillips

ISBN 978-1-7323935-6-1

Cover Design
© 2020 by Kayla Esther Ciardi

Mongrel Empire Press
Norman, OK

Online catalogue: www.mongrelempire.org

This publisher is a proud member of

COUNCIL OF LITERARY MAGAZINES & PRESSES
w w w . c l m p . o r g

Acknowledgments

My thanks go first to God, with whom all things are possible, and then to the women who did the work. Rilla Askew, an amazing author and editor, who was kind enough to read the manuscript, believe it should become a book, and then proceed to set that process in motion. Jeanetta Calhoun Mish, poet and publisher of Mongrel Empire Press, who also believed in this work and physically transformed the idea of a book into reality. Ellen Stackable, my friend, who has long listened to my voice and sought a way so that others could hear it as well, setting the fruition of a dream in motion. This book owes its existence to the three of you. Thanks is such a small word to express my deep gratitude and appreciation for all you have done, yet it is the word I have. Thank you.

I would also like to thank the myriad volunteers of Poetic Justice OK, both those I have had the pleasure of meeting and working with (Hannah, Abbey, Cyndi, Meg, Teagan, Julie, Sarah, Maggie, Mary, Karen, and Liz) and those I have not. This book was seeded in the rooms of writing, friendship, and acceptance that Poetic Justice provides. Thank you for changing the world.

And lastly my sisters of the locked boxes: Angelina C, Sheree A (my beta readers who unwittingly convinced me to keep writing—one with tears and one with "what happens next?"), Kelsey D, Cheryl W, Michelle M, Brandi M, Sophia C, Nayeli C, Felicia R, LaDonna W, and many others—far too many to list. I want to thank you most of all for sharing your years, lives, laughter, and love with me. You made the unbearable somehow endurable and gave me a reason to be grateful. My love loves you always.

Slightly altered versions of Albuquerque I and Albuquerque II were first published in *Columbia: A Journal of Literature and Art*, Issue 57, Spring 2019. http://columbiajournal.org/

Contents

This book is for my children

and

in honor of the 12th Step
which is "to carry the message
to those who still suffer,"
and the message is this:

There is hope.

Disappearing In Glimpses

Foreword

Perhaps she stood by the side of the road, watching as you passed by.

Perhaps she served you lunch where you spent more on your meal than she would earn in an entire shift.

Or you brushed by her in the aisles of a library.

She sits somewhere right now, in an anonymous building that you have seen but never known is a shelter for victims of domestic violence, a homeless shelter, a trap house.

Or she is looking up from a prison yard in the fly over zone as you pass over her. She is watching your plane on its way to places she has never been and cannot go.

Wherever she is, wherever you are, you both exist simultaneously. You either have met her or you are about to meet her. Your destiny is about to collide with hers.

Perhaps her world did not begin in dirt roads and muddy rivers but instead is steeped in urban concrete and stained alleys.

Because although this story is my own, it is an archetype. A template. The most common of stories among the most common of people.

The poor. The lost. The unseen.

So, you will meet her. Will you see her?

Or will she simply be a disappearing glimpse fading into the white noise of your day.

She is the same girl no matter where you meet her.

Will you be the same?

—Geneva Phillips, 2020

Personal Archeology

A handwritten excavation
inky brushstrokes unearthing events
as singular revelations
fragments bear bleak evidence
crystalline etchings
verbal accusations scarred into surfaces
  withheld from affection
reassembling dysfunctional bones
into their secret skeletons
tracing thoughts back to a common
Alcoholic.   Abuser.   Ancestor.
painstaking reconstructions
once stoic profiles shattered
hand carved cameo decorations
formerly engraved upon
memory palace gates
  Now fallen to ruin
lost in briar jungle
reclaimed by red sands and clay

dirt floor shack   greywood porch
sagging
        dogskulls   stare down
blind knotted faces
spill pinesap tears
      leaving dry bumpy runnels
dust mote eyes cast about
watching tongue lash cuts
      catch betrayal in splinters
Behold, thorn clad regrets.
Oh, crown, you have no place here.

back and betwixt
    forward and forth
I remove pieces, cataloging
discoveries and relative remnants
            precisely I record and
reorder chaos

assigning numbered spaces
                containing between pages
time
    is a cushioned compartment
    which holds still and has no end

it's confusing, my friend says,
over a phone that rustles
    crinkling restless dollar sounds
and clinking cents fall
like each word tossed
    down the line
distance is an echo
splashing in my ear

So is life, I want to tell her,
and faith.
so is love.

Instead

I am plucking loose,
I am fingerbraiding
  a single thread of hope
        thin as a strand of hair

Can I spin it into gold?

1. Barefoot *Early 1980's*

She ran barefoot all summer. School let out in May and she shucked her feet like early corn, stripping off dirty, hole riddled shoes and pulling away thin mismatched socks. She gazed thoughtfully at those two white feet. Pale. Unfamiliar. Unblemished and tender.

She ran barefoot down pencil drawn trails, arms spread wide in a balancing act. Cool dirt track hard beneath newly exposed feet. Shadow-dappled deer a fleeting curiosity glimpsed from the corner of her mind. Skyshine. Sundrunk. She fell onto damp banks, elbows planted in bed soft moss. She caught at thoughts that streamed through her head gleaming. Clear and elusive, able only to retain them in swallows like the water she drank in between reckless and brave daydreams.

She ran barefoot through whipping, heavy-headed grass, and over crunching, crumbling carpets of old leaves. She ran barefoot through patches of stickers and stood wobbling on one leg while pulling those tiny, clever weapons out with quick jerks before she could lose her nerve.

She often stubbed her toes, tearing off great hunks of skin and meat. Her mother doused such injuries with rubbing alcohol, peroxide, or fiery orange Merthiolate and told her, "Wear your shoes." But she never did.

She ran barefoot through murky brown puddles of water that collected in the deep ditches lining both sides of the road. She ran barefoot through thick red mud and by the end of summer her feet were as hard as the rest of her. Equal parts sun and dirt. Even her dark tangle of hair and intense watchful eyes held hints and echoes of that red clay. It entered her mouth, stained her blood, and sank through her bones. When she woke each morning, she smelled of hot iron, copper, and hazy plumes of red dust.

At the end of summer, she would hide her feet away once more, encasing them in rough canvas cocoons purchased at second-hand stores and yard sales.

Forgetting them as they transformed slowly, back into those strange, soft things that could never belong to her.

2. Dimensions *2012*

She lies awake. Uncomfortable, she shifts on the bunk. Her bones clink and tinkle, old dusty bottles shuttering on a shelf.

Her memories are matchsticks which she strikes against the darkness. Old stories and ghosts remembered or repurposed. Reconstructed from the limited reflections of her perspective. Fluid dimensions of Once, Then, When, and Now. Traveled into, through, and between by breath, thought, or dream. She vanishes and reappears in glimpses.

The only place she cannot reach is forward into the future where she grows indistinct, uncertain, and diminishing. Still, she tries and in trying, she becomes an indistinguishable ending in a search of a place to begin.

3. Pills *2009*

She makes a study of dying. She adds to it layer by layer. The dishes are piled high in the sink. The bathroom is filthy. There is not a clean article of clothing in the place.

She grew up in filth and said she'd never live this way, but here she is, too far down the rabbit hole to turn back now. The only way out is through.

People are afraid to die. She finds this tiredly ironic. To her, death is the last bastion of welcome. A weary hope of surcease, an absence of pain. The only promise left that matters.

There are white pills and yellow pills and dark rust red pills. She swallows them all. Sometimes she throws them up and wakes in pools of dissolution and vomit. Sometimes she wanders out and someone calls an emergency responder. Then she wakes in the hospital, psych unit, emergency room. Restrained saline solution revitalizing neglected systems. Momentarily too preoccupied to remember what she is so desperate to forget.

That suppurating spiny pit where her motherhood once resided. Judged and terminated, parental rights severed, and with them all her hopes. Tied, clipped, and burned in a belated sterilization performed freely by the state.

Nurture center forcefully lobotomized. Diagnosed and medicated. Grief unrecognized. Spiritual trauma dismissed.

Now she is what they made her out to be. Careless and unfit. An addict. She takes the drugs because she cannot take the pain.

The silenced patter of tiny feet and laughter are the empty ringing echoes that drive her to oblivion.

Where are her children?

No one will tell her.

They are being held for an unspecified ransom that no one seems to know how to pay.

Too late, they say.

She takes the pills they give her and some that they don't.

She sleeps and sleeps.
To forget how to scream.

She has forgotten how to live.
So she keeps trying to die instead.

4. Brownies *2003*

The little boy sits on the counter. His long hair is tied back. Dark gold spirals shine softly against the red backdrop of his t-shirt.

He watches the rhythmic beating of the batter as if hypnotized. *Whap. Whap. Whap.* The wooden spoon picks up the rich, thick brown batter, scraping against the bottom of the bowl and lifting it to the top before folding it seamlessly back into the center.

Two cake pans are oiled and lightly floured, set to the side. Two tiny feet dangle naked, occasionally kicking a heel into the cabinet door.

A heavy clear glass bowl rests between mother and son.

Whap. Whap. Whap. Whap.

She gives the sides a good scrape, beating it a few more times. The only lumps left are the pecans. His curious eyes follow every movement as she dumps half the batter in one pan, the rest in the other. With rapt fascination, he studies the way she smooths the batter flat and then squeezes liquid caramel over the tops of the raw brownies in careful lines before using a butter knife to zig-zag it prettily before sliding them into the hot oven.

His heels *tap, tap, tap* against the cabinet door while his eyes find the bowl that now sits empty on the counter.

She takes the wooden spoon and chases stray batter down with it until she has a heaping dollop. She hands it to him, comically gigantic in his small hand, a movie set prop.

He opens his mouth wide, sticking in as much of the spoon as he can. Sticky chocolate batter instantly smears each side of his mouth. His eyebrows climb high and two deep, deep dimples appear, carving their permanent charming marks in both of his cheeks and her heart.

Innocent sable eyes meet hers as he declares with all earnestness, "Mom! You should win a trophy for that!"

She smiles. Her heart as warm and full and sweet as the smell of brownies in the kitchen.

"You reckon?" she asks him just to hear his answer.

Nodding his head solemnly, he replies, "Yeah, Momma, I neckon."

5. Leaving (1) *1984*

Beneath the soles of her shoes, the dirt road is comforting and familiar. She feels the velvety soft dust shifting loosely around the perpetual rocks with each step she takes. It helps to focus on the familiar.

It is scary in the dark. She has been down this road hundreds of times, but it seems totally different now, leached of color and company. The moon is high and bright which helps some, too. At least she can see.

She has dumped the belongings out of her mother's purse and filled it with her own meager possessions. She wears the long strap crosswise over her chest.

The trees are windbusy, lining both sides of the road. Their full summer leaves provide background noise for the night that is alive with locusts, tree frogs, and crickets. The volume is amazing, but comforting as well, these sounds have filled her nights all of her life.

The dark hills block out most of the stars, but a bright swathe is cut above her and she follows it as much as the road.

She is forsaken.

She fell asleep in the living room and woke with her father's hand between her legs. She never thought he would do that. Everyone else she had come to expect it from. She'd grown used to it and the dread-filled shame that came with it. The only girl with half-grown men for uncles. She'd been taught from her earliest memories that it was just what boys did and it was all girls were good for.

Except for her father. Her daddy. Her dad. He had always been different. He never touched her that way. He never would. Until he did.

He had stopped suddenly, jerking away when she turned over and looked him in the face. Even in the semi-darkness, she could see the fear in his face, watched it smooth out flat into a mask on a man she didn't know. In silence, he got up and walked normally back to the bedroom he shared with her mother.

She had lain there not knowing what she should do.

She was sick with dread and shame. This betrayal was more than she could bear. The knowing that now, there was nowhere she would be safe from hands and eyes that demand too much. Prying away from her with ruthless determination things that she doesn't want and doesn't know how to give. She is twelve years old and she cannot remember a time when this was not true.

She doesn't know what time it is. She is exhausted. She leaves the road making her way through weeds and bracken onto the brushy boundary where county land gives way to private property. A rusty barbed wire fence punctuates the clearing, standing sentry over nothing but long grass. She lays down using the purse as a pillow.

Sometime later, she wakes. All the stars have changed their positions, but reality has not.

6. Leaving (2) *1992*

She has packed two changes of clothes in a bag. Cigarettes, make up, and a gold chain she has stolen to pawn in Tulsa when she gets there.

She has track marks and bruises all over her body and she does nothing to conceal them. The world has failed her at every turn, and she hardly cares if society thinks her a failure. The thought grimly amuses her with its inevitable irony.

She walks and hitchhikes.

She is offered $20 to give a blow job, and it is the first time she's ever taken money for it. Desperation has made her a grudging participant in her own exploitation. She gets out of the truck feeling dirtier and lessened for it. She refuses to think about it. She packs it away with everything else that doesn't bear thinking about. One day that space will be too full and the door will not close anymore. But for now, it does, and she lights a cigarette standing at the entrance to the onramp outside of Sallisaw.

She is homeless and hopeless. Rides come easy, with or without strings attached. Funny how women never stop for a woman. Only men. She is used to it.

She lived in Tulsa before when she was a ward of the court for 3 or 4 years. Downtown feels like coming home, or as close to it as she can get.

She has nowhere to go and knows no one. She walks around until she just can't walk anymore. She buys something to eat and sits down on a bench. The day is warm and nice. A late afternoon golden haze covers everything, and if she didn't know better, she might believe the air of well-being it seems to promote. She wonders if she can sleep here. She is worn out all the way through and has no idea where she can spend the night. A rough looking black guy approaches her. He strikes up a conversation, bums a smoke and tells her if she'll buy him a couple of beers, he can show her a place that she can stay. A shelter. She buys the beer and walks with him over the railroad tracks. He tells her don't worry about remembering how to get here. This time of day you can just follow the homeless. And indeed, they practically materialize out of the very dusk the closer they get. He walks on to the Day Center for the Homeless while she takes a place in line for the Salvation Army. She is admitted. Receives a sandwich and a bed.

She has stumbled upon a dull fragment of relief, a wretched benediction. Another low rung of survival, her next step.

7. Fireworks *2002*

Twilight gives way to night with the slow shedding of a bright blue silk robe revealing the ripe, velvety plum truth beneath.

Boat lights reflect off the dark water like floating gems scattered to tempt mermaids.

The boats crowd the surface of the lake. An accident seems imminent. Lively whoops and drunken yells echo over the expanse.

Her daughter sits on her left side, head leaned against her shoulder, yellow cast enveloping the arm cradled in her lap. Evidence of an unhappy childhood lesson in the effects of climbing plus gravity. Her waist-length sunny brown hair brushes the natural rock outcropping. Tangled strands are tugged fitfully by the soft erratic breeze, becoming long tendrils caressing the air.

Her middle son sits to her right. Small and snug against her side. Sleepy eyes watching for the first explosion of color.

On her lap rests the youngest. Ever silent and content, he stares at the boats. Autism as yet undiagnosed.

She has always loved the water. She grew up with clear running creeks and a red muddy river. Everywhere she's been since, from Austin to Tacoma, she has found herself drawn to the water. She loves the wet-green smell, the fleshy slap of wavelets against the shore. She loves the closeness of the gathering night, babies held safe, sharing time that even now is solidifying into memory.

She shifts her weight in search of a more comfortable position. All three children shift accordingly. The first fireworks rise over the water. Long comet tails fizzling colors, igniting, they burst into sizzling patterns of light. Green, blue, red, gold. Hollow booms reverberate through the air, the night, their chests. Fiery shreds of paper, disintegrating into ashfall, blowing over and even onto the boats. The burning snow of summer.

She watches her children as they watch the fireworks. Reflected glories flashing across their faces. She reads wonder and awe in their wide shining eyes, their soft open mouths.

She engraves this moment into a memory surface. She stamps it into the fabric of all she is. She finds expressed in this rare glimpse, so uncommonly clear, made beautifully perfect, her reason for existing.

8. Albuquerque (1) *1993*

She is living in Austin. She has left behind a son and a needle habit. She is mourning one and trying to replace the other.

He's been stealing cars since he was 13, he tells her. He is 19 now. She is 21. They arrive in Albuquerque in a stolen white Trans Am with a blue T-Bird on the hood. The car kept overheating the whole way.

They sell it at a chop shop just outside the city. They hitchhike into town with all their bags and rent a room at a cheap motel called The Gaslight. She likes the name. It makes her think of Victorian London in the middle of the desert. That makes her smile.

He is caramel colored with short jet-black hair he swears is brown when it's long. He has deep, deep dimples, and when he smiles it is the sun breaking through the clouds that cover her heart.

They stay on the Res for a while. The Isleta Indian Reservation is all adobe and sand. A casino sprouts like a modern mirage from the vast xeriscape. There is no work and no weed. Before long they hitchhike back to town.

At the welfare office she applies for food stamps for both of them. The caseworker is an old white man who tells her interracial relationships never work out. Her eyes burn stark and sudden. All the things she keeps closed up in her mouth march across her face. The old man approves her application without another word.

They walk past a Planned Parenthood clinic. She takes a pregnancy test. It is positive. They are happy, silly kids with a kid on the way. Everything seems bright, different. She doesn't miss the drugs. She's found something better.

For a long time, she thinks it is love.

9. Albuquerque (2) *2004*

They have 3 kids and a pit bull living in a kitchenette. They are at the same motel they lived in when she was pregnant with their daughter. Back then it was called The Desert Rose. Now it is the Tin Tan Apartments. It is smack-dab across from the pink stucco wall of the fairgrounds. A cheap by-the-night haven for heroin junkies, crackheads, and prostitutes.

She has followed this man around for eleven years now, the father of her children, from bad situations to worse. This might be the worst. They are barely making it. They both work for the owners making one-half the weekly rent each. He works maintenance at another motel. She cleans rooms at this one. Daily she finds crack pipes and crumbs strewn everywhere. Sometimes needles, which she throws quickly away.

Her children are unhappy. Tired of moving. Here they are made fun of for their unfamiliar accent. Better here to sound Mexican. Beans and fry bread are the main staples of their diet. Plus whatever free food the Indian Center is passing out, whenever she can make it down there.

One day her daughter comes in from school telling her about a man exposing himself to her and her friends at the bus stop. Thankfully her son has no idea what has happened, but her daughter's innocence has been damaged. She is only nine and a half years old.

Now she walks them every day back and forth from the bus stop. It is only two or three blocks, but she has to leave her youngest, who is autistic, alone while she does. And while she cleans rooms. She shouldn't. He shouldn't be alone with the TV babysitting him. There is nothing else to be done. She cannot forgive herself for failing her daughter. She has always promised herself that their childhood would not be her own.

Her children are sad, and she hates it, but she does not know how to fix it.

She is sad, and she hates it, but she does not know how to fix it, either.

14

She thought they could start over here, but it seems like no matter where they go, nothing gets better.

He has left them twice, now, for someone else and it seems all he ever cares about is having things he thinks are cool and smoking weed. They aren't kids anymore, yet he says he'll never grow up. She feels so trapped by her love for this man. Is this what love is supposed to be? She doesn't know anymore.

It is such a relief when her mother tells her on the phone that they can come and stay with her in the house she is buying. Her mother has left her father after thirty miserable years. She doesn't want to be her mother. She doesn't know how not to be.

Finally, she thinks, a chance to get out of here and do better. Start over. She goes into the bathroom and takes the glass pipe out of the wall where she has had it hidden these last few weeks. She wraps it in toilet paper and steps on it. The crushing glass feels final, yet temporary at the same time. She flushes it all down the toilet.

They load everything into a white Oldsmobile Cutlass. The sun is setting as they leave. She watches shadows pooling under the scrub pine on the mountain behind them.

The car overheats the whole way back to Oklahoma.

10. Systems (1) *2005*

She sits on a bench in front of the windows overlooking the courtyard.

She wears a long floor-length skirt and a nice blouse. She holds a book loosely in her hands.

She is homeless, but it no longer fits her. She avoids conversations. Someone is always trying to talk to her, to feel her out, see if she is down to do whatever. She wants no part of it. She's just staying here until she gets a job. She has to figure out how to get her kids back. He has left her again, dumped her off in Tulsa and kept the kids, moving them with him into his girlfriend's place. She has made her way to Oklahoma City to be closer to them. Even though he has told his family that she abandoned them. He, of course, wants to be the hero. Much easier to win the support and sympathy of relatives when you're a victim.

A man with a briefcase keeps walking by her. He is dressed casually, but not street casual. He also doesn't look like he belongs here. She knows that doesn't mean anything. The City Rescue Mission is filled with every imaginable type of person. Mental health patients, prostitutes, families displaced by alcoholism and domestic violence, drugs, and unemployment, and gangbangers fresh out of prison. She's even seen one man who reminds her, remarkably, of Jimmy Carter slumming or possibly looking for Habitat for Humanity applicants.

The guy with the briefcase stops in front of her and asks if she'd like to talk in his office. He tells her he is a representative for a mental health clinic. He is friendly and personable. He offers to set her up with an appointment at the clinic.

She doesn't want to be on medication. She feels like she is going crazy, and she is afraid if she doesn't do something soon, she is going to hurt herself. She doesn't want that either. She just wants her kids back. She asks if he can help her with that. He says he can't. She is waiting for her appointment. She sees the man almost every day. Sometimes he takes her to get something to eat at McDonalds. Once they went to a Chinese buffet, and she watched people on TV wading through the chest-high water of Hurricane Katrina. That is what she feels like. Like she has been hit by a hurricane and everything is gone.

One day he asks her if she'd like to go see his house. She thinks, probably she shouldn't. But they are friends now, and she hasn't had a friend in what seems like forever. They take a drive. There is a prescription bottle in the console. It is not his, but he tells her she is welcome to take some if she wants. Hydrocodone. She takes one and then he is pulling into a gas station on the way, asking if she'd like something to drink. She hasn't drank in a long time, but so what? What difference does it make now? There is only fear and pain and emptiness where there used to be a family. She has to forget, it's the only way to survive.

He buys her something to drink, and they are at his house. He is cooking dinner, and she is drinking. She doesn't know what to make of this, but for now she is not sad or thinking of her kids. And this is the first time for either of those things since she became abandoned.

Later she gets sick. Unused to the alcohol or pills. He lets her sleep in his bed, and she wakes with him curled around her, pressed up against her. She knows, instinctively, that he is waiting for a sign that she is willing. She is not, but cannot move away from him without shifting and probably sending the wrong message. She lies very still and hopes he will not ask for more or take it.

She falls back asleep and wakes slowly and half hungover. They drive back to the city like all this was normal. Unfortunately, for her it is and will continue to be.

He tells her that once she is on medication, there is a better place she can stay than the Rescue Mission. Also, that there are all kinds of programs and resources available to help with an apartment and transportation.

She understands using the system and all she has to do is to take the pills they give her and go to her doctor and case manager appointments.

She thinks it is not much of a price to pay and it isn't, at first.

11. Systems (2) *1985*

She runs away, but they keep sending her back to the group home.

It's not that she hates it. She doesn't really. It's clean and bright and most of the people who work there are pretty cool. It's just she doesn't think anyone—any grown up—has the right to tell her what to do. Where were they when she was little and needed help? Who are they to try to tell her what to do now? She can take care of herself. She doesn't understand this place or these people.

All she wants is to go home. For her mom to believe her. For them to go away somewhere else, without her dad, and be a family.

But that isn't happening. So she runs away. One time she picks up a gallon of bleach and chugs it like the beer and whiskey she's learned to drink. It won't stay down, though, and it hurts even worse when it comes back up. They send her to a mental health unit for three days after that, but they let her go back to the group home.

She hates the school they send her to. She skips it and spends all day downtown at a big library reading.

She's never seen so many books in her life. Sometimes someone will pick her up and smoke some weed with her. Then she wanders around downtown stoned.

She likes watching the clear water in the reflecting pools and all the strange people waiting for the city buses.

She sits down outside when the days are nice, watching the water and the people. The endless sky with only tall buildings to block out the sun. She likes downtown Tulsa. She thinks it is a big city.

Sometimes grown men approach her. Usually she gets a bad feeling and won't go with them. Once or twice she's had to go into the library and hide because they won't leave her alone even after she tells them no, she doesn't want to go with them anywhere. They just keep offering her liquor or money or asking what she wants. She's 13 years old. She just wants to go home. She never says that, though. She knows that isn't what they mean.

One time at night, when she was running the streets AWOL from the group home, she came upon this van in a parking lot with a man and a couple of women in it. They called her over, and she went to see what they wanted. They are smoking a joint on the end of some hemostats and pass it to her, and start telling her how they are like gypsies. Just traveling around the country in their van and she should come with them. She has taken a couple of hits off the joint, but it is not enough to dull the bad, bad feeling she gets when she thinks about getting into that van. They say they are going to Florida or California or even New York if she wants to go. And all they'll do is party the whole way. She says no thanks and takes off with them calling behind her to come back. She hurries away and down some twisty turns through alleys wondering how many kids have gotten into that van and what happened to them.

There is a boys group home a couple of streets over from the girls group home she stays at. One night, a few of them all go AWOL together, running the streets, breaking into cars in the parking garage. They find sixty dollars in rolled up nickels in a cigar box and a gun they don't take. They wait for the liquor store to open at 10 the next morning. One of the boys is 17 with a deep voice and a full beard. He goes in and comes out with a brown paper sack full of fifths of whiskey.

They go to a basement in an old abandoned house in the neighborhood. All of them go to the QT to get some cigarettes except her and this boy she likes. He is 16. She is the youngest in the group, always trying to prove how cool she is. She downs the whole fifth in 5 or 10 minutes. She doesn't remember anything after that. She wakes up at the group home. Someone went and got a worker when she was unconscious and began to choke on her own vomit.

They tell her she has quit breathing twice, and that she is going to be sent to a lockdown treatment center for teenagers. She finds it hard to care except for having to leave the friends she has made. It is just one more step down a road where no one knows or wants her.

They do not know what to do with her. They are sure she is going to end up killing herself either on purpose or on accident.

19

She can't blame anyone for not wanting her around. Her own family doesn't. No one loves her and she hates herself for that and everything else. She must not be worth loving. She wishes everyone would just leave her alone. They won't let her go home, and they won't let her die.

She can't understand why.

This life is not worth living, anyway.

12. Systems (3) *2007*

The facility is large and reminds her, from the outside, of a drug rehab or community-type prison. On the inside it is more like a hospital.

This is where her youngest son is. He was taken from his father's new wife's custody while his father was in jail. Since his other siblings were already in DHS custody, he was placed in it also. His siblings are at the Indian Children's Group Home in Muskogee. They have been moved multiple times before finally being placed there.

This is the J.D. McCarty Center for Children with Disabilities. Her son has been placed here because of his autism. She is supposed to get to visit her children once a month by DHS policy. Since they have been placed outside the county, DHS is supposed to provide the transportation and supervision. She has only been taken to see them every 3 or 4 or 5 months. The visits are always being rescheduled.

This is the second time she has gotten to visit her youngest son since he was put in DHS custody several months ago.

He is so big. He has lost his two front teeth and his permanent teeth are coming in. They look mismatched and awkward in his little boy face. He has her big dark eyes and her dark hair. He is the only one who looks just like her. She's always called him her forever-baby because of his autism. He is 8 and still non-verbal, but he is so smart.

He sits on her lap and they play old games, tactile, touch, and sound. She sings him the theme song of his favorite cartoon, SpongeBob SquarePants. And on the last long draw out, "PAAHHHNNTTSS," he tries to cover her mouth with excited movements.

She touches his short hair and is fascinated with the sprinkling of new freckles on his face. He is light like her and his brother, but without the epicanthic folded eyelids of both his siblings.

She will get to visit them next. They'll drive on down to Muskogee and she'll get to see them for an hour or maybe two. Then she won't see any of them again for months. The drive takes twice as long as the visit, and afterward, all she has to look forward to is never-ending court dates and regularly postponed visits.

It is time to go, and she does not want to leave him. She sits him down, and he knows she is leaving. He takes her hand and tries to go to the door with her. She cannot do this. She stuffs her heart someplace dark and far away. She has to put his hand down and tell him, no he can't come. Her tears are choking her, but she says it and keeps them inside. She doesn't like for the workers to see her cry. They don't care, anyway. They always look at you like you're doing something wrong, no matter what you're doing.

These people are killing her. And there is nothing she can do except leave her children where they are being held. She looks out the window of the car so the worker can't see her crying.

She is taking the classes and the drug counseling and the drug tests even though she was sober when they were taken. Not even smoking weed. Just the psychotropics the mental health clinic had been giving her.

She has been taking the classes for over a year. First one place and then another. The judge colludes with DHS. DHS is always making up excuses or stories as to why they've done this or that, like moving her son and daughter 5 times in one month. The judge takes DHS' side at every turn.

She has no one except a court appointed attorney who will never speak up for her.

She keeps doing everything they tell her, but the one thing she's learned from all these classes is that no one with money ever loses their kids.

Only poor people, like her.

13. Leaving (3) *2009*

She packs a bag, has her purse, puts on some good shoes. Shoes she can walk some miles in. She has a fifty-dollar money order he has given her to go pay his court costs while he is at work.

She has left before. Many times. Somehow she keeps coming back. Stitches in her face. X-rays. Broken windows. Trashed apartments. He's choked her unconscious twice. She doesn't know how many times she's had him put in jail. This man. The artist. Domestic violence shelters, crisis centers, and back to Tulsa once for several months. Somehow she keeps coming back. She thinks at least part of it is that she deserves it. For failing her kids. Losing them to DHS. For not being a good mom. Two years of doing everything they said and still she managed to lose them.

She had started college at OSU at OKC convinced, somehow, everything would work out alright even after being terminated from the classes she was in for showing up with two black eyes and half her face blue and green after he'd head-butted her in the face. She'd tried to say it happened playing basketball, as unlikely as that was, but one of her classmates told it was her boyfriend and everything fell apart even though he was in jail. This time for a year.

So she started school. Had an apartment. Thought it would be enough. But it wasn't. They terminated her rights while she was at school one day. She didn't even know she had court. No one notified her.

Now all she has is this. This man with his pretty face and lies. This charming drunk with his hidden vodka bottles and rage and fists.

She can't do this anymore.

She pulls the locked door shut behind her. Another cheap by-the-week room. All they can manage to stay in these days. She walks the short walk to a check cashing place and cashes the money order. At the Greyhound Station she buys a ticket to Tulsa—goes in the bathroom and snorts her last Ambien. She knows if she doesn't, even now, she might go back. The Ambien helps. Some. She wishes she had another.

23

By now she is up to 300 mg of Effexor XL a day, 3200 mg of Neurontin, and 10 mg of Ambien a night, but those rarely make it through the first 24 hours of getting her prescription. Still, she thinks she's sober. Been sober for a while. Can't drink with him or one of them is going to end up dead. The cops keep telling her that, anyway, and she's coming to believe it. No money for anything else. Just barely enough for her cigarettes and his vodka.

She goes outside to smoke and the huge bus pulls up rumbling out the great cloud of diesel exhaust. She loves that smell. It smells to her a comforting mixture of distance and safety.

She hauls everything on the bus and picks a seat by a window in the back. All the landmarks are like signposts to her now. Oklahoma City falls behind and with it the last vestiges of hope. Of getting her kids back. Of somehow things ever being okay again. She knows now, it will not. She's glad to leave that relationship behind. The worst addiction she's faced so far. Even now, as Tulsa draws near and the sedative effects of the Ambien wear off, she can feel that terrible tenuous stirring of guilt and responsibility which she has so debilitatingly misplaced in that man.

She pushes it back and away.

Someplace dark and forgotten.

The bus pulls into downtown Tulsa. It feels like coming home or as close to it as she's ever known. She lived here for years when her kids were small. Working at a Goldie's through both her pregnancies with the boys. She is here. She feels a rare feeling almost like freedom except for the shadows of loss and hopelessness that cling to her everywhere she goes.

She's been thinking about this guy she used to go out with the last time she stayed here. He was always good to her. Different. A hustler. She wonders if he's still around. Wonders if he still gets high. Wonders if anything can make her feel not so lost and broken. The medication isn't doing it. It just keeps her afloat in a sea of unending misery. She has to find a way to survive this pain. Somehow. She doesn't know if she can.

14. Darker *2010*

She shoplifts compulsively. Stops drinking after a trip to the hospital sends her home in paper clothes and humiliation.

Her wide eyes hide the lies, the truth, the dangling hangman's noose. She has become an expert at dodging questions and concealing answers. She loves him as much as she can, but can't remember the first time she told him so, blacked out on methadone. Spends a weekend high and steals some jewelry from his girlfriend's house. Gives it away as friendship tokens the next day.

She has a habit of self-destruction she can't kick. She burns strange patterns of scars on her arms with cigarettes. He watches as she takes too many pills and sees all the holes in her the needles can't fill.

She tells him she's a gypsy, and she'll never marry. The truth is she can't believe anyone will ever love her and not leave. Especially a hustler like him. She calls hope a sickness and she inoculates against it with remedies that regularly vary. She is careless with her words and money. She brews fresh coffee at midnight in between hits from the pipe. Late one evening, she claims to know what love is, but can only recite what it isn't. When she's not high, she reads books thicker than the stack of pancakes she makes for breakfast. She hides poems in his pockets when he's not looking. She loves him more than she's ever loved anyone in her life, but can't tell him. She knows she is too broken to be fixed, so she runs away from the things in her heart. She knows her feelings are dangerous, so she pretends there aren't any. She sits naked in the chair high on Xanax watching football. She blesses her Tarot cards before she shuffles them. Doesn't know the difference.

There is never enough to fill up the emptiness that is consuming her. Days turn to weeks, she can't recall or remember. She wanders away in June, doesn't call 'til November, without looking back. Still, he took her back because he loves her, too. But she just keeps getting darker.

15. Shots *1996*

Her mother is driving. Her daughter is secured into the car seat in the back. She has the window rolled down and a cigarette hanging out of it.

They are on their way to the Leflore County Health Department to get her daughter caught up on her 2 year immunizations.

It is Friday. She is off work from the cracker factory everyone calls the bakery. The day is nice. Black-eyed Susan and wild daisies nod dusty heads as they pass. Blackberry bushes are late blooming and honeysuckle blows in the warm air. Shady tree-covered corridors usher them onto the blacktop which leads to town.

Early summer is her favorite season. The sweet-grass smell of growing things scent even the dust that billows in their wake.

She dreads taking her daughter for these shots. It makes her upset and irritable. She is short with her mother as they pull into the parking lot. Her mother is pragmatically implacable as usual, slamming shut the rattletrap car door and heading briskly to the entrance.

She unstraps her daughter from the car seat and hoists her into the familiar position on her hip. Shoulders hunched, head down, she trudges across the concrete slowly entering well behind her mother and signs them in.

She has to have her shots her mother tells her as they wait in the hard plastic chairs for the nurse to call them back.

"I know, Momma," she says tiredly. She does know, she just can't bear for some stranger to hurt her baby. It has never been okay to her, but everyone else thinks it is perfectly acceptable.

Her mother sighs with well-worn resignation. This is not the first time for this discussion or what comes next.

The nurse calls them back and they all three go down the hallway to a small room with barely enough chairs.

26

She sits the baby on her lap. A bright-eyed, brown-skinned, chubby little girl looking around happy, curious, and unafraid.

She starts crying silently. She can't help the tears that overfill her eyes. She tries to blink them back, but they run down her face instead. Her mother gives her a disgusted look.

"You're just going to scare her," she says, "Look, she's not scared or crying."

"That's because she doesn't know what's going to happen. I can't help it, Momma. You know I can't do it," she says quietly as she continues to cry.

"Give her to me," her mother says tersely.

She hands her over just as she always does.

The nurse comes back into the room with two hypodermic syringes and the bright pink plastic packet of the oral polio vaccine.

Oral first, then swab the leg, stick, cry. Swab the arm, stick, cry. Her cries sound of pain and betrayal.

She looks at the floor the entire time, unable to watch. After it's over, her mother hands back the baby. She cuddles her close trying to comfort the both of them the best she can.

Her mother sighs, "I don't know what's wrong with you," she says as she turns the key in the ignition.

She doesn't answer, just lights a cigarette and blows a heavy plume of smoke out the window where it disappears into the uncaring air.

She looks in the side mirror at her daughter's face, tear tracks still visible on her chubby cheeks.

It's my job to keep her safe, she thinks, not let people hurt her. Why doesn't anyone understand that?

16. Failed *2006*

They sit outside a convenience store on the south side of Oklahoma City. She has called the police and she holds the protective order that has a handwritten directive from the judge that her youngest son is to be remanded from the kids' dad to her custody immediately. They are waiting now for the police to bring him to her.

Her daughter and middle son are in the back seat. They are playing with the big stuffed SpongeBob that was to be their brother's Christmas present (past) and now his welcome home present. It is good they are together again, but there is still a piece of their small family missing and it is an ever-present hole in their lives. But everything is going to be alright now.

The children ask if the police are going to bring him soon. How much longer, they want to know.

"We just have to be patient," she tells them, turning around in her seat and lighting another cigarette.

She is glad to have them back. She finally feels like there is hope. It is a scary feeling, a feeling that invites disappointment, but still a good one.

She'd gone to the big library downtown and gotten on a computer. She put in the password for his email, and he hadn't changed it yet. Everything was emptied except a draft of where he'd requested some tax credit check be sent to his new address.

She wrote it down and then looked it up on MapQuest. She was going to get her children back one way or another. She waited until she knew they would be out of school for the day, then went to the house. Her daughter and middle son were the only ones there. The woman he was living with had taken her youngest son with her someplace. The kids' dad was still at work.

She asked them if they wanted to come and live with her. They said yes. She told them to go get in the car. No shoes. No clothes. Nothing.

She'd get them whatever they needed. She'd been putting things up for them for months already.

Later that evening, she called his mother to let someone know that they were okay, they were with her, and she was keeping them. His mother screamed into the phone, "You can't do that! You can't just take them!" She hung up while she was still protesting. They had all betrayed her and thrown her away. Pretending she didn't exist and kept her kids hidden from her. There would be no sympathy now.

The police came and checked to make sure the children were safe and well. They asked if the kids wanted to stay there. They said they wanted to stay with their mom. The police went away satisfied. Since then, she'd been going to Legal Aid to get full custody. They were helping her, and she worked during the day at DHS, dropping the kids off at school, and picking them up in the afternoon.

The police car pulls up. Her son is not in it.

They tell her that no one would open the door and that an order from a judge is not a search warrant. They could not go into the house and take him. She should go home now, they say, there's nothing they can do.

The children can't understand why he isn't coming to live with them like she told them he would. They are quiet and sad in the back seat.

"It's just *not yet*," she tells them, starting the car and putting it in reverse. She looks in the rearview mirror but can only see the stuffed toy discarded on the seat between them.

17. Leaving (4) *1987*

She hasn't been home since she was twelve, hasn't lived at home since she was eleven. She is going home now. The state of Oklahoma is through with her.

She spent over a year in lockdown treatment facilities. While she was there, her mom and dad came a few times for visits, family counseling, and a couple of day passes. Her dad admitted in family counseling that he had molested her.

Somehow she'd believed that if that ever happened, if he ever told the truth, it would be like a magic wand. Everything would be fixed. Her mom would leave him. The state would let her go live with her mom. Everything would be okay.

That is not what happened. The family counseling session ended. Her mom and dad went home. She stayed locked up. Nothing changed.

After a year of state-paid-for-treatment at this facility, they said she was done. They sent her back to the same group home she'd been at before.

She promptly ran away again, this time with another 15-year-old girl, and they spent a couple of weeks hitchhiking with truckers before ending up in Houston, Texas.

She saw Chicago, Pittsburgh, Lafayette (Louisiana), and the Atlantic Ocean. They drove through a tunnel cut right through a West Virginia mountain. Endless miles of cornfields in Ohio, the flat "Bluegrass" of Kentucky, and Memphis, Tennessee.

It was one big adventure. The truckers were nice. Most of them probably had kids at home around their age. They fed them and bought their cigarettes. It was probably the first time in her life no one tried to or made her have sex with them.

They got to Houston and called her uncle. The first night all was well. They smoked some weed that looked like hay, her uncle told them was Jamaican Gold.

They left his house the next afternoon and went wandering around. They got picked up by a couple of black guys, got drunk on 6 point beer, ended up getting raped at a park.

Her friend called her uncle to come get them. He did. The next morning a big burly lady sheriff came and roused them out of bed, cuffed them up, and took them to Houston's Harris County Juvenile Detention Center. They were there about a week before Tulsa DHS arranged for them to be flown back.

She is too broken to be easily fixed—they are sending her home instead. She is sitting on a bus waiting to leave, staring out the window. A guy in his twenties asks if he can sit next to her. She doesn't care. They make small talk.

She is tired. They came straight from the airport to the bus station. The group home had already packed up her stuff in cardboard boxes, and they are with the luggage under the bus.

She falls asleep. She wakes up with the guy against her back, hands groping her. She lies still.

She wonders if this is how it will be all her life. One man after another trying to stick something in her.

He gets up and gets a blanket out of the overhead. He covers them both with it. He is fumbling with the button on her jeans. She lets him undo it. She has learned it is easier to just give in. It is all she has known.

18. Crank *1988*

She has moved out of her parents' house. She is kicked out of high school permanently, they tell her.

She lives part time with her friend's parents and part time wherever she ends up.

She meets a guy who is 21. She thinks it's great. He has some money from getting hurt on a sandblasting gig, is old enough to buy liquor, and smokes weed. It is all she aspires to do. Be altered. She doesn't like the way she feels when she's not.

She ends up living with him, and he introduces her to crank. He buys a gram in a little brown glass bottle. She doesn't like snorting it, but she likes how it makes her feel. She doesn't need to eat or sleep. She thinks it's like being a demigod.

They start going to Texas to buy it from a guy he knows there. She begins wrapping hers in loose twists of rolling paper and swallowing it like a pill. It tastes like poison if she doesn't. They drive all over selling it. There is no shortage of demand. She no longer drinks or smokes weed. There is no need to. One time she doesn't sleep for fifteen days, and they stop at a motel. He is in the shower, and she sits in the cheap chair by the table. She starts dreaming with her eyes open. It's the longest she has stayed up, but she knows some people who've stayed up thirty days. They are usually not the same after that.

They go to a house in Fort Smith to sell some dope. There are a lot of guys there. They buy some crank and turn a pop can upside down. They dump it into the depression at the bottom of the can. One guy pours some water in it. They all have syringes or are waiting in line to use one. They surround the can reminding her eerily of an array of malign butterflies. Steel proboscises extended. She knows this is a terrible thing she is witnessing. She never wants to be one of these people.

She goes out to the car and twists up a bump in paper, swallows it without soda. She has come to like the chemical taste it leaves in her mouth. She lights a cigarette and waits for him to come back out. They are supposed to be driving straight back to Texas after this stop.

He brings one of the guys out with him. It is someone he went to school with in Keota.

She climbs over into the back seat. She'd rather ride back there anyway. She won't have to talk. Just be alone with the chemicals in her head.

19. Staying *1989*

She is pregnant. She stops getting high and checks herself into a juvenile shelter. She can still do that with her mother's signature since she is 17.

She tells him they have to quit getting high. She won't come back until he stops the crank. He brings her flowers and says he will.

She stands on the porch smoking and remembers how she was at this same shelter when she was 12.

It seems like she has lived a lifetime in those 5 years.

She arranges for him to give another girl a ride from the shelter to Sallisaw. She doesn't hear from him for a couple of days and figures he is with that girl getting high.

When it gets dark, she goes out on the porch to smoke and takes off. Leaves all her stuff, hitchhikes to the next town over where she used to go to school. She finds a party, gets drunk, hooks up with this boy she used to know, and starts making out with him.

They end up leaving the party together. The sandblaster pulls up as they are walking to another house. His cousin is driving. He gets out and grabs her, pushes her into the back seat. He is pissed she is with someone else, she is pissed and drunk. They fist fight for miles in the backseat while his cousin drives on the backroads. She starts kicking his cousin in the head to make him stop the car. She can't fight anymore. They go to the motel he's been staying at. She has a black eye and a concussion. The alcohol is wearing off, and she just wants to sleep.

He tells her she looks pretty with a black eye. He won't let her go to sleep until she lets him have sex.

This is the easy part, she tells herself. But it's not. It never is.

They go get her stuff the next day. He quits selling crank and using it. They get an apartment in Fort Smith, Arkansas. She stays.

Waiting for the baby to come.

20. Failed (2) *1992*

She pushes the pills out of their plastic bubbles one at a time. They are blue over-the-counter sleeping pills. She has bought several boxes. 80 pills. Surely it will be enough.

When she has them all out, she takes them one at a time. She is sitting in the bathroom of her friend's house. She thinks she might throw up before the last few are down, but she chokes it back and her stomach settles.

She throws away all of the trash and puts the glass in the sink. Goes into the bedroom and lies down on the bed to wait. She is hoping to go to sleep and not wake up.

The sandblaster has taken their son and disappeared with him. Her mother has even taken her looking for them. No one will help her. Not the police or DHS. They tell her possession is nine-tenths of the law. If he has him, he can keep him. If there is no court order to determine custody, she is screwed, basically. If she can find him, she can take him back, they tell her. It goes both ways. She cannot find him.

She did not know it was possible to love one small person so much. She cannot live without him. She wasn't a good mom, she knows this. She couldn't be. She was unable to function without some combination of chemicals to alter her.

She left her son with friends to go out partying. Really, her friend's parents, the same people she had lived with off and on for years. She was shooting dope now and would stay gone for a few days at a time, but she always came back. She knew he was safe and taken care of, even if she wasn't there.

Now she doesn't know where he is and his father doesn't take care of him. He only took him because she won't go back to him this time. She is done with him, and he knows it. The only thing he has left to hurt her with is her son.

She falls asleep but wakes up in the hospital. They put a tube up her nose and down her throat. She tries to fight them. Someone keeps

35

asking her if she knows where she is. What her name is. She doesn't know what she says.

She sees strange things that she knows isn't right, but they seem real at the time.

A person she knows is dead, she sees pushing a wheelchair down a hallway. A boy she went to high school with is wearing a lab coat looking over a chart. Her mother is there and her brother. She is not sure if they are real or not. She can't tell.

She doesn't know how long she's been here. They are telling her she is going to a mental hospital in McAlester. Her mother is going to take her. She signs the papers they give her. She wonders if she will always feel this way now or if it will wear off. Everything seems surreal.

She doesn't know if she likes it or not.

They tell her she has been in ICU for 3 days. She almost died. She doesn't know why she didn't.

In the car, they don't talk. Her mother has the radio on.

She stares out the window and cries. She still doesn't know where her son is. She misses him.

21. Systems (4) *2002*

She sits in the Muskogee mall. She's sure it has a name, but she does not know or care what it is. She won't be here long. She's just waiting for her brother to come pick her up.

It is high summer, and she leaves the food court for outside. She needs a cigarette.

It is beautiful out. She has just spent three weeks in the Muskogee County Jail and outdoors seems at once a luxury and a necessity (it was the longest she'd ever been in jail and she hadn't actually been in jail for years and years). She cannot get enough of the heat, the sun, the fitful wind. She watches old people walk past her, tracksuits and bright white tennis shoes. Mall walkers. She cannot understand why anyone would choose to walk indoors on a day like this.

She is anxious and restless. She is desperate to get back to her children. Before this, she has never been away from them all, not even overnight.

They are at their dad's aunt's house.

Everyone is mad at her. His aunt, her own parents. She can't blame them. She had just got a job. A good paying job. She'd only worked one day before the 4th of July holiday weekend came and he called. Wanting to take the kids to the lake like they did every year. Their family tradition. Even though this year, they were separated. Him living with his girlfriend, her and the kids with his aunt.

He was already on his way when he called. It was a moment's notice. She shouldn't have gone. She wants him back without really knowing why. She wants her kids to have a father, but it's more than that. She can't bear to be cast aside. Even though things aren't great, not even good really. And haven't been for a long time. She doesn't want to lose him, her family, her sense of security and identity, so she went.

There was no reconciliation at the lake. He made it plain he just wanted her there to help with the kids, to cook. To make it feel normal for him and the kids. She never would've went if she'd known. Too late now and all for nothing.

They left late in the evening. Well after dark. They were pulled over in some place called Beggs. Some hick police chief who thought he was John Wayne. All they found in the car was an empty marijuana pipe. They acted like it was a pound of meth.

They took them both to jail and took their kids and put them somewhere with strangers. His aunt wasn't allowed to come get them. They told her she had to wait until DHS court and see what the judge said. All over an empty marijuana pipe.

The car didn't have seatbelts, and they charged her with "permitting child abuse by allowing children to ride in a vehicle not equipped with seatbelts." Gave her a $200 ticket for "allowing an unlicensed driver to operate a motor vehicle" even though it was his car, not hers. And a misdemeanor charge for the empty marijuana pipe.

She sits in jail for 21 days. At court she pleads guilty to the felony even though her court-appointed attorney advises against it. He tells her they can get it dropped to improper child restraints—a ticket—if she can just "wait it out". She cannot wait it out.

They are setting next available court dates for October. Her family will not bail her out or get the car out of impound—they are punishing her for her bad decision.

She cannot sit in jail 3 months. The kids' great aunt will not keep them that long. She knows she is lucky they are with her and that she's even kept them this long. She has to get out. She agrees to a year's supervised probation, gets a DOC number, and a child crime. The DOC website will list her crime as "beating or injury of a child." She will be shamed by and grievously resentful of this injustice.

Her only consolation, such as it is, is that she and the kids' dad have reached a tentative reconciliation at court dates and through illicit jailhouse notes. He will fight the charge. His court is set for October. She will take the felony and get out to get a job and make a place for her and the kids, a place for him to come back to.

She has no idea what she is doing. She is just frantic to salvage what little she can. Not to lose what little she has. Even at this price, any price really. Just to be able to keep him, her kids. Just to be able to pretend someone loves her a little while longer.

Her brother pulls up. She climbs into the cab of his truck. They don't talk much on the drive. Listen to Linkin Park, smoke cigarettes. He drops her off and she goes in the house. Things are awkward, tense, off kilter.

The kids are happy to see her. She is profoundly relieved to be back with them. Her youngest has been severely traumatized from this whole ordeal. He won't let her go to the bathroom without him, and wails inconsolably if she leaves his sight.

That night after she finally gets them to sleep, she just sits listening to the sounds of their sleeping breaths. Her daughter snores a little. The boys breathe almost in tandem. They are the most comforting sounds she knows, but there is little comfort to be found. She is sorting and packing their things. They have to leave. His aunt told her after she got back from getting groceries. She handed her the food stamp card back and told her a cousin would be there before noon to take them wherever she wanted to go.

They have nowhere to go. She has a check for her one day of work. Enough for a motel for one day. She'll have to find a shelter to take them within 24 hours or be on the street with 3 kids.

She sorts, folds, discards. Listens to the breathing.

She never knows what to keep, what to throw away.

22. Sampson *2003*

Something inside her is broken. It will not heal. The edges just keep grinding, grinding together. She thinks it might be hopelessness.

She tries to do what is right. They are staying with some friends of the kids' dad, a couple he went to high school with. They have four kids who run wild. She has three of her own. The woman works and is only there when she's sleeping. She makes pretty good money and works as much as she can. The man doesn't work. He and his friends just hang out all day smoking weed, playing video games, and hitting golf balls into the trees.

When the woman gets paid, twice a month, they both go to town and blow her whole check on themselves. Fast food and games, electronics, beer and weed. Hardly any groceries. Never any dog food.

Once a month the man will drive to the tribal headquarters and pick up a load of commodities. They last a week, 10 days at best.

There are three pit bulls chained up around the house plus a little dog that stays inside and their own pit bull.

She goes to town whenever their food stamps and money run out. She shoplifts large packages of lunch meats and cheese. She buys a loaf of bread usually with change. If she has two or three dollars she buys some cheap bags of chips. She feeds all the kids and the adults, all manner of mooches and bums. Friends and relatives of the people they are staying with. She has gotten good at stealing. She's had plenty of practice since they began living here.

The dogs are slowly starving to death. Not her dog or the little one, but the three outside. She is keeping the kids from going hungry. She does not know what to do about the dogs. It is breaking her heart. Two of the dogs are crazy from being on the chain, but not Sampson. He is a good dog. A good boy. He's been retired from fighting by one of their friends, and he is supposed to be bringing dog food out as payment for them keeping him. But he's strung out and there's been no food for a long time.

He is a big dog with a massive head. But his body is a wasted skeleton.

40

She cannot stand it. She searches every cabinet for something to feed him. All she can find is a couple of cartons of commodity oatmeal. She cooks up an entire container, takes it out, and gives all the dogs some. She gives Sampson the most. Nobody cares. They don't care if she feeds them or not. They don't care if they die or not. They just keep bringing in more dogs that no one will care for.

Three tiny puppies appear. She feeds them bacon grease because there is nothing else.

She goes to town and steals ham and cheese, roast beef, bologna, big family packs of all kinds of meat to feed an army of children and grown men who do nothing but smoke or drink themselves into stupors.

She cooks giant pots of pinto beans, lima beans, kidney beans, and takes them out to feed to the starving dogs. She wasn't sure, at first, if they'd eat plain beans, but they do. They gulp them down in great steaming heaps.

One day she and her middle son are sitting on the steps outside the side door. Her son is holding a kitten in his lap, one of the newest cute and forgettable animal acquisitions to arrive. Sampson comes around the corner dragging his huge logging chain.

She would like to just let him go. Surely he would have a better chance on his own, or someone would have pity on him. These thoughts have plagued her for weeks. She knows though, if she did, there would be hell to pay. They have nowhere else to go until they get a car and can get a place.

So she keeps trying to feed him, it's all she can do.

Her son is petting the kitten. Sampson smells it and then leans in and grasps its head between his great jaws. With inexorable gentleness, he pulls the kitten slowly from her son, as if he doesn't want to alarm the kitten and make it scratch the boy. She tells her son not to look. She covers his eyes with her hand, and watches as Sampson crunches the kitten's skull in his mouth. One of the men come and take it from him, flinging the small body over a barbed wire fence and out into an empty field.

The men laugh and joke how that dog hates cats, but she doesn't think so. She thinks he just wanted something to eat.

Later, before Christmas, she is picked up on a warrant. She spends New Years and most of January in jail before it's all said and done.

When she gets out, Sampson is gone. He starved to death, her kids' father tells her. She knows it is her fault. She is the only one who cared. She should have been there. She could have saved him. At least kept him alive a little longer.

She feels defeated by the relentlessness of life. She wonders if anything she's ever done has mattered at all or if everything is just postponing the inevitable, terrible conclusion.

23. Joy *2005*

She is staying at a place called the Jesus House. Her friend who works for the mental health clinic got her in.

She has to take meds, but it's not that bad, 10 mg of this, 20 mg of that, 100 of Neurontin, which she has to switch from nights to mornings because it gets her high and she can't sleep on it.

The lady who did her diagnosis said she couldn't tell if she was bipolar depressive severe or if she was clinically depressed with PTSD. They go with bipolar.

When she was a juvenile, they diagnosed her with a borderline personality disorder and when she tried to kill herself at 20, they said she had mild to moderate depression. She's learned to just go with whatever they say.

She can't go anywhere for the first 30 days and all new residents must attend AA meetings every night in the dining room. Thirty meetings in 30 days. They hand out one pack of cigarettes per person per day and give her a job in the warehouse sorting stuff and putting together food baskets. They put out all kinds of free stuff and people park and line up down the block to come in. She likes the work. She likes that they help people. Everyone is pretty nice and she's always getting cool clothes, good stuff, shoes and purses.

She didn't know what to expect when she first got here. People on the street at the other shelters told all kinds of crazy stories about this place and at first she was wary of staying here. But it's cool. Plenty cool. She doesn't mind the meetings in the evenings. She used to have to go to NA meetings when she was in treatment as a kid.

The people are a trip, though. All kinds of people stay here. Sometimes she thinks they're like characters out of a bunch of crazy stories all mish-mashed in here together.

There's the good looking ex-bull rider who's getting sober off alcohol but takes a lot of pills for pain. A crazy ex-teacher who chain smokes cigarettes and asks her if she can find her any books on horses. She only likes books about horses! There's a lady who's been here for like 10 years who doesn't take any meds, thinks the showerheads are microphones, and will only sign her name as an *.

There is this goth-guy who does really good impersonations over the loudspeaker system at night and a toothless old black man who wears a lime green jacket and calls himself The Reverend.

There's a couple of young black guys who are both handsome and running from something. And a middle-aged black guy who runs the warehouse and has a dog named Boo.

All manner of alcoholics trying to get sober, junkies trying to get clean, and every single one with mental health problems all living together, working together, and somehow fitting together into a cohesive unit, with plenty of dysfunctional codependent relationships sprouting in the night like doomed mushrooms.

It is all right up her alley. She fits in almost seamlessly. She likes it here rather well. She is doing good.

Her friend from the mental health clinic comes and visits her regularly. They never talk about what happened before. She sorta picks up one of the black guys (or lets him pick her up) even though he's at least 10 years younger than her. He's nice. His face lights up when he sees her, and for a while, it's enough.

One day they announce that there is going to be a big convention downtown, and they have tickets for her and a couple of the other women residents if they want to go.

Several of the women staff members will be attending. Does she want to go, they ask. She wants to know what it is, and they tell her it is the Joyce Meyer Women's Convention. She is a Christian speaker who is famous all over the world, they say.

She has never heard of her. She's never had any use for the Christian religion. All she's seen is rich white people showing off their money or crazy Pentecostals falling out with oil on their hands and foreheads. She doesn't care for it either way.

She's read some stuff on Buddhism, had a fascination with paranormal and metaphysical studies, owned a pack of Tarot cards most of her life, and looked into a couple of polytheistic religions, but she's never known anything about the Christian religion other than she's basically against anything the establishment endorses.

But these people are really nice, and she still can't go anywhere else for a couple of weeks. So she says yes, and the next day they all go downtown to the Cox Convention Center.

There are a lot of people there, mostly women, a lot of sale booths set up inside, and she registers this as authentic American Christian capitalism, but she's never seen anything like this and can't hold on to her normal level of cynicism for long.

The music starts and everyone is standing. She stands, too. She is mostly watching the woman who is singing, looking around at the people. There is a liveliness in the atmosphere she is unfamiliar with. But she feels it. Feels the inexplicable, benevolent presence that caresses her like a cool breeze.

She looks to see if there is an air conditioning vent close by, but the ceiling looks like it is miles away, so it's not that.

She continues to feel it, and then suddenly, it is inside of her. This light. This joy.

Never, in her entire life, has she felt joy.

Before this moment, she would have sworn it wasn't even real. That it was just a sham people put on to make you think they had some magical, great life.

But this is real, and she is utterly amazed.

At once she understands that her entire life has been lived as if she was profoundly deaf in a hearing world. Watching people around her responding to music she could not comprehend. It is as if the whole world has been singing, dancing, exulting, and rejoicing to this music that she not only couldn't hear, but was unable to believe was real.

Now she can hear it. For the first time in her life, she knows what joy is, feels the ineffable connection to all that was, that is, that will ever be.

In an instant, she knows that hope is a gift, not the curse she has ever believed it to be. She understands inherently that God is good. She can feel it all the way through because it is inside her.

She doesn't understand how this has happened, but she never wants to let it go. She has been changed in an instant.

She is a believer. She has been baptized with the Holy Spirit, and she never could have believed it was real if it hadn't happened to her.

She is on fire for God.

She goes back that evening and it's like she's a new person. The guy she's been messing with has a Bible and he gives it to her. A white leather King James Version. She reads Proverbs, Psalms, Ecclesiastes, and the New Testament. She has never had any desire to read the Bible before today.

She has been brought to life, and she wants this new life more than anything.

Within a couple of months, she's traded the one black guy for the other one. The Jesus House people have helped with a car and helped her furnish the apartment she got through mental health funding. She reads every version of the New Testament she can find.

One day the Holy Spirit prompts her to log on to her kids' father's email account. She goes and gets her daughter and middle son.

In the car, she tells them, "Fear not little flock for it is the Father's good pleasure to give you the kingdom" (Luke 12:32).

At the apartment they ask her, "Momma, are we rich now?" They are awed by the nice things and all the stuff she has been putting away for them, sure that she would get them back. "No," she tells them, "God did all of this for us."

24. Friends *2007*

She is still in the same apartment as when she lost her kids.

It feels empty and abandoned. It used to feel as if she were waiting for them to come occupy the spaces she had prepared for them. Now it feels desolate.

She is filled with restless apprehension. It never goes away. She takes more and more medication. No one ever tells her there is no cure for grief. They just keep increasing her dosages. It is not enough.

There is a knock on the door, and she opens it to find the woman who gave her children over to DHS custody standing there.

The woman tells her she is glad she still lives here and how sorry she is that she called DHS. She just couldn't cope and she didn't know what else to do. Can she forgive her? She's been at a rehab called First Step and it was an awful work farm. She just got out and has nowhere to stay.

After the initial shock of seeing this woman again wears off, she lets her in and quietly considers what she's told her. She knows it's true. The woman couldn't cope, obviously. Not even for a week. She's already had 4 or 5 of her kids taken away by DHS and every time she has another one, they take it at the hospital. The woman is on far more medication than she herself is. The last time the woman stayed with her, she'd just had a new baby and it was still in the hospital. They went to visit once before the state took it. Once you've lost your kids, it seems they put some kind of flag on you and if you have more, the hospital informs DHS so they can take them, too.

She has just begun the long process of trying to get her own children back. She keeps signing up for classes. Domestic Violence and going to meetings, but DHS keeps telling her to wait. The court has to order the plan so that all the classes can be paid for at the places they require her to go. So, she has to wait.

She looks at the woman. All the anger and resentment she has felt for her in the past months has evaporated. She realizes she has forgiven her with a tired, resigned sort of forgiveness. The kind of forgiveness that is resolved to the fact that every effort is doomed to failure, so what difference does it make.

She tells her she can stay for a while until she figures out what she's going to do.

It is a terrible idea.

She is tired of waiting. They start going to a Mexican bar on the Southside. She starts drinking again. There is a lot of free beer and free cocaine. They go to the bathroom and do lines off the back of the toilet.

Her friend has had several kids with Mexicans, and although she actually looks more Caucasian, she can speak Spanish fluently.

They drink, party, lose the car, go find it the next day parked here or there, once stuck in a giant pothole in an alley.

They argue, go their separate ways, apologize. They are bound by the unifying factors of loss, dysfunction, and addiction. This is the foundation of their friendship. The woman is a raging alcoholic and once she starts drinking, she doesn't stop. She becomes terrible, volatile, unbearable.

When her friend buys cheap wine from the liquor store across the street, she often leaves the apartment. She can't deal with it. She doesn't want to drink every day. She prefers binges, drugs, and sleep.

When they are sober, they occasionally go to church. The big mega church she used to take her kids to. They were all supposed to be baptized there together. But it never happened.

She listens to the praise and worship. She still feels the presence of the Lord, but it seems like a distant, unobtainable thing now. Like sunlight on a storm-wracked day. Sometimes she weeps for it, but she doesn't know how to get back all she's lost. She's only ever known how to survive, not overcome.

She knows everything she's felt for and about God is real. That what has and is happening has not changed reality. But she does not know how to get back to that place of joy and peace. Where she is now feels irreconcilable.

She clings to the promise she made her daughter at their first DHS supervised visit. They stood in an empty conference room, a row of windows behind them showing the sun glinting off row after row of parked cars.

She hugged her, hugged them both, and looking into her daughter's dark red-brown eyes, she promised her she would not give up. Ever. No matter what.

She has broken every promise she has made in her entire life, but she will not, cannot, break this one. She holds to that promise and a thin thread of hope, they are all that bind her to this life.

One night she leaves her friend drunk and crying on the couch. She walks, and hitchhikes, and ends up in some Mexican apartment run by the Cartel. The guy whose name the apartment is in likes her. He tells her to come back later by herself. She gets dropped off down the street at a store. Walks back. They sell cocaine out of the apartment and keep money for pickup, 30, 40, sometimes 50 thousand dollars at a time. They pick up coke in ounces from one of the many Mexican run garages. It is all cleverly done. Not too much dope in one place, the money is picked up like clockwork. They keep the money stacked inside a box spring in the spare bedroom. A lot of Mexicans coming and going, no one pays any attention.

She is gone for six days high on crack. Him and her are the only ones who smoke it. Everyone else snorts powder. No one shoots it.

She is exhausted, says she needs to go home, get some sleep. He gives her a car to drive. She stops for gas, has trouble getting it restarted. He told her it's not stolen. She doesn't believe it. You have to turn the key just right while holding it in gear before it will start. Finally, she gets it. The sun is a glaring red hot poker in her gritty red eyes. A branding iron in her brain. On the highway, she watches people's faces in the cars as she passes them. How bright and shiny their lives look compared to her own.

She thinks about jerking the wheel to the left. Smashing into an oncoming truck. Head on. The car is very small, surely it would kill her.

The truck passes. A man driving a little boy in the passenger seat.

She looks back at the road. How can she let her misery collide with someone else's life? It's not right. Besides. She promised. She wouldn't give up. No matter what. Killing herself is the ultimate give up. She can't do it.

She pulls into the parking lot of the apartments, passes the dope boys on the stairs. They are young, cute, always trying to pick her up.

She reaches the apartment door not sure what she'll find inside. Her friend still drunk? Passed out finally? Gone?

She flicks the light switch on, but it doesn't banish the darkness. She brings it inside with her.

25. Leaving (5) *2005*

It is the first day of the year. Last night was their eleventh anniversary. They went out to the VooDoo Room in Tulsa. A long drive from her mother's house in Leflore County.

She didn't dress up. Didn't wear makeup. Didn't really drink. He doesn't like her to do those things. He doesn't like guys looking at her, and they do, whether she's made up or not. Still, he doesn't like her drawing attention to herself.

They went to see some washed up eighties rappers. She was never a fan even when they were controversially famous way back in the day. But it was alright. Afterwards, the rumor spread, there would be an after-party at the Adam's Mark Hotel. They decided to go. Went to the floor everyone agreed was the right one. Nothing seemed to be happening. The two of them went down a floor or two, walked the hallways, still nothing. Outside one of the hotel room doors, they see a suitcase. He asks should he take it. "Grab it," she says. It is purely spur of the moment opportunism.

They get out to the truck, throw it in the back, and leave.

Her mom's house is two hours away. They pull off the highway, get the suitcase, open it. Inside they find a male masturbation device, which he quickly discards with a cry of revulsion, some clothes, a file folder containing information on horses, basketball games, and other stuff for betting on, and 28 1-gram baggies of what she thinks is cocaine. She pours some on a cd case, makes a line, snorts it. She hasn't done coke in 13, 14 years (except for what she smoked in Albuquerque, and he doesn't know about that and never will). Her nose and throat go numb. "It's coke," she tells him. They pour some in a joint. It goes oily, hard to keep lit. It tastes weird, but not really bad. They are high. Horny like teenagers, they have sex in the truck right there on the back road. Drive home.

No one wants to buy the coke. They all do homemade meth or ice down there. They sell a little, snort the rest. He gives some to his brother who sells it and re-ups with ice from a Mexican their cousin is living with. They've already been selling weed, now they start buying a couple of pounds at a time (one to sell, one to smoke), and selling ice. Smoking it, too. She learns how to make a pipe out of light bulb and a straw. Feels like MacGyver.

Things start getting weird. His brother and him can't really handle the high. She used to do crank way back when, and she can see they are edging out of control. She tries to tell them they should all stop smoking it. They all need to stop before bad things start to happen. She sees the end coming, but no one else will stop, so she doesn't either. Their relationship teeters one way and then the other. First they seem closer, obsessed with each other, with sex. He works nights and she drives to spend his lunch hour with him. They get high together. She gets high alone when she gets back. Becomes an expert on glass. She gets the kids off to school. Sees them when they get home. Makes sure they eat. Take baths.

Stays high.

After 6 months of this, he is seeing someone else. She's been through this twice before, so she knows. This time, though, is the last. He has warrants and she knows where they are staying. She faxes all the information to the local police department in the town they're at. Turns out, the kids' dad and the new girlfriend both have warrants, dope, a stolen highway patrolman's state-issued revolver, and a quarter pound of weed.

Her middle son is there. She and her mom go to pick him up and get the truck.

His brother is keen to keep on selling. She starts going down there. Giving him rides back and forth to Tulsa. They've always been friends. She thinks they still are, but the ice is taking over. They have an argument after she drives 10 hours round-trip to Lawton to pick him up and then take him to Shawnee and drop him off. He gives her $20 for gas, and she throws it on the ground. Leaves.

The kids' dad is calling to her mom's. Wants her to bail him out of jail. Doesn't know she's the reason he got picked up.

Since her son was there, the cops are keeping her informed on the progression of the case. She goes by the station one night, and they release a list of pending charges to her. This is a mistake—they're not actually allowed to do that, and a lady detective is later pissed about it. Wants her to return it, but she doesn't. There are about 20 felonies listed. Plus, he's been to prison twice before. Once in Oklahoma before she met him and in Washington state where their daughter was born.

It was his new girlfriend's apartment and she is out of jail the next day. They both made deals. Roll on three, go free, they say. He is released out of that jail, but has a warrant, and is transferred. She bails him out of the second jail. They fight over her showing the list of charges to his brother. All of his friends. Everyone knows now. You don't just walk away from a list of charges like that.

She has bailed him out with money she has stolen from her mother. She feels awful. She didn't mean for things to turn out this way. She left the bank card and a note to keep the monthly deposits until it's repaid, but she knows he will just get the card cancelled now that he's out. Everything is in his name. He's made sure of that.

Now that he is telling her she can stay here in Holdenville with his friends. Her and the kids. He's going to stay with his girlfriend in the next town over.

She cannot do this. She cannot do this. She has given everything up for him. All these years, and now even her family, to do whatever he wanted her to do. Now he is telling her he is going to live with this girl still, while she sits here with 3 kids, no job, no home, nothing. She tells him she can't.

She has nowhere to go. He knows it and does not care.

He won't let her take the kids if she won't stay here. She can't have them. Even though he's the one who is wrong. He still will have his way. She gets nothing.

"Just take me to Tulsa," she says after sitting in the truck all night crying. He keeps everything. The kids, the truck, a place to live. He loses nothing.

It is summer. She has one pair of shoes on her feet. One suitcase. She tells him to throw everything else away. She gets a motel room for 3 days. He gave her a couple hundred dollars out of the five he pawned the computer for. The computer that's not even paid for that she took from her mom's.

A 3-day reprieve and then the shelter again.

She has nothing to show for the last decade of her life.

Just this devastation.

She can't imagine what comes next.

She cannot conceive of any good thing.

26. Insanity *2011*

The spoon is on the table. Handle bent to create an angle needed to keep it flat and steady. Orange caps lie discarded. Clear tube with flat black plunger, pin prick silver tip gleams malevolently, seductively. Just a tool to use productively.

Dark-brown liquid cooling, cradled in the bowl of the spoon. A drown chamber pooling, hoping she'll wade in soon. Calling for her to cave in. All she has to do is give in. It's never hard for her to lose this game.

She drops a scrap of filter and it flutters down. She takes the needle and sticks the tip in, presses it down. Pulls the plunger back, back, back, a little more. Til it's 60 thick, black as molasses. This is the hit she dies for.

Her man sits across the table. The light is good. She doesn't have to tie off. Finds a good vein right off. She's supposed to stop at 30, but she pushes it all in and places the spent rig next to the spoon still on the table.

Next thing she knows, she's staring at the ceiling fan and the light is too bright. He tells her not to get up, says if she does, he'll kick her head off. She doesn't know he's just restarted her heart. Given her mouth to nose resuscitation. She was blue with her jaw locked, but he pounded, pounded, pounded on her chest til she took a breath and brought her back from the dead. She gets up anyway.

The spoon is on the table next to the straight glass pipe and rock still laying there. She says, "I need a hit." Seating herself back, she loads the crack and flicks the lighter. Always, she is always trying to get a little higher.

She couldn't stop and even after it killed her, it could not slow her down.

The spoon is on the table.

27. Sounds *2012*

The sound of prison is yelling. It is swearing. It is the sound of a fist hitting flesh and the silence of onlookers. It is the sound of childhoods lost to broken violence, ground glass despair. It is . . .

"CHOW TIME!"

"MAKE A HOLE!"

"FIVE MINUTE MOVEMENT!"

It is doors locking and unlocking so regularly they become a part of her circadian rhythm.

It is learning people's names at mail call while listening for her own.

It sounds like sockets popping, showers running, noodles being crushed in plastic wrappers.

It sounds like sliders closing, dominoes hitting a table.

"LOCKDOWN FOR COUNT!"

It sounds like continual complaining about the food, the guards, standing in line, the weather, the guards, canteen, property, standing in line.

Breakfast line, pill line, lunch line, library line, toilet paper line, dinner line, church line, microwave line.

It sounds like kicking a hacky sack, serving a volleyball, bouncing a basketball, hitting a softball.

It sounds like rap music, country music, pop music, heavy metal, and Christian music. Arms raised in worship, heads bowed in prayer.

Hearts lifted in hope, even as years disintegrate into dusty red sand under tired feet standing in line.

28. Systems (5) *2012*

Razor wire and chain link fencing. It's all she sees the first year. Every time she thinks she has hit a bottom, the bottom drops out, and she finds herself even lower.

She doesn't think things can possibly get any worse than this. Prison. An 18 year sentence at 85%, which means she'll do 15 flat calendars, or so proclaims the new lingo.

Her public defender brought her the paper to sign, told her, it's not a life sentence. She looked him in the eyes and with tears running quietly down her face, she said, "Yes, it is." At forty years old, what else could it be?

She tries not to look past the fence. The fence is acceptable. It is the new hopeless boundary of her existence. She is okay, if she only looks at the fence. It is when she looks past the fence that she feels what little sanity she's regained slipping. Freedom, trees, and fields, and a whole world. Everything she still loves or ever could love on the other side of that fence. Gone. All gone, gone, gone. And in 15 years, what will be left? What could be left? Nothing. Nothing at all.

So, she's trained her eyes to not-see. Not see the trees. The wooded hills. The fields. The road leading away. She only sees the fence. The razor wire. This is reality. This is where reality is contained. A few square acres. For all intents and purposes, the rest of the world does not exist to her just like she does not exist to the rest of the world.

She owns 3: 3 pants, 3 t-shirts, 3 smock tops, 3 panties, 3 bras, 3 pairs of socks. A wool blanket, 2 sheets, a towel, a pillowcase with no pillow. She receives $5.00 a month as a Level 2. She is supposed to receive an indigent pack with hygiene supplies, but they are always out. So, she buys hygienes with her $5.00. It is not enough to buy shampoo, soap, conditioner, toothpaste, and deodorant. Never mind envelopes, stamps, paper, pen. She should get envelopes, paper, and several free letters a month (postage paid through the mailroom), but rarely do they supply even this. She gets one roll of toilet paper a week, like everyone else, and 30 of the most cheaply produced sanitary napkins she's ever seen. Too bad if you run out.

She didn't know what to expect. She'd never been to prison before, had never given it much thought. Now that she's here, she knows what to expect, but she still doesn't know what to think. This place is crazy. The people here are crazy, and the people who run this place are crazy. The only difference between them at any given time are the color of their clothing and one group gets to leave at the end of their shift while the others don't. Ever.

The one thing that's become abundantly clear since her inception into this pseudo-world, this sub-sub-culture, is that they don't want anyone to leave, ever. The only people they let out are the people who've already been in and left two or three or half a dozen times. They only let out the ones who are most likely to come right back. Everyone else, the general consensus concedes, is screwed.

She sees 20-year-olds with 35 year sentences at 85%. She never heard of the "85% Law" until she signed for her time. This whole corporate-minded infrastructure (aka the criminal justice system) wasn't even on her personal radar. Until it was. Until she was here. Swallowed into the leviathan of all systems. The great beast of incarceration.

Mostly poor people end up here. There are some people with money, or whose families have money, here. But, the majority of people here are varying degrees of socioeconomic poverty. The disenfranchised, she's learned they're called. A lot of addicts, a lot of people with mental health issues, a lot of people who made some bad decisions for one reason or another. And a few killers. A few out and out sociopaths, but not many. Not many at all. Certainly not enough to qualify over 1,000 women in this one long-term facility.

There are virtually no programs. Especially if you've got a long sentence and already have a GED. Faith and Character is about the only program available, so she signs up. God knows, she's low on both.

She's off all medication, has been since right after she got here. She's sober, clear-minded for the first time in she doesn't know how long. She doesn't know how she feels about it. She likes the clarity, the daily lucidity of it, but she does not like the yawning emptiness and hopelessness inside her. She feels like she is walking a tightrope over the precipice of all her dangerous feelings and one slip could undo her.

It is hard to adjust. Even for someone whose life was total chaos and dysfunction. This place is traumatizing. Standing in line for hours to eat, to get meds. Fist-fights breaking out in lines every day. It's one of the reasons she got off the medication, that and the fact that they just kept trying her on different things she couldn't take, and she was sick of trying to escape the inescapable with the paltry chemicals they were offering her. She has trouble sleeping. It's hard sleeping surrounded by the unknown. All these people are strangers and many are strange, indeed.

There is no control in this environment. The people who are in control are inconsistent at best and add to the confusion, sometimes purposefully or out of general incompetence. They yell, swear at the inmates. Call them either "bitches" or "ladies." She thinks this an ironic reflection of the male perception of women boiled down to its base.

They are herded one way and then the other. To dining, from dining, packed in hallways, lines and cells. Called "offenders" or "inmates" on every piece of paper she can see.

Despite all this, it is hard for her to stop thinking of herself as a human being.

29. Apart *2010—2011*

She is sitting on the couch next to him. The morphine has given everything a warm, fuzzy, golden glow. He is watching TV. She is watching him. She loves the smooth, dark satin of his skin. The stubble on his jaw, his eyes, his lips, his smile.

She is thinking something she knows is dangerous. Questions are dangerous things. Answers can be worse.

Before she realizes it, she is saying, "If I asked you to marry me, what would you say?"

He looks at her with his dark eyes. She can never tell what he is thinking. He doesn't say anything for a moment. Even with the blurred edges of the morphine, she begins to feel apprehensive.

Finally, he says, "Are you askin'?"

She loves this man so much. This hustler. She never wanted to love any man ever again, and she certainly never planned on falling in love with him. She used to tell him "don't get too attached" before she went back to the city. But she came back. And now she's too attached. She loves him more than she's ever loved anyone.

Is she asking?

She can't imagine what it will feel like if he says no. Better to leave it alone. Better to keep what she has than ruin it with an answer she won't be able to get over, she thinks. She lowers her eyes and covers the disappointment with resolve. She looks back up, voice tinged with something that might have been second thoughts, she says, "No, I'm not asking."

She lays her head on his shoulder, holding onto what she has.

✳ ✳ ✳

They are high again. It seems they are always high these days. He is putting some stuff in a bag. Clothes to take to his friend's house. Things are going south with the apartment. There's been trouble with the people over the rent. Eviction is eminent. They are getting by on borrowed time, and they both know it.

He is saying that if they get married, they can stay at a shelter. Together. Usually men and women are kept apart at shelters unless they're married. Then you can stay together, but you have to have a marriage license.

She stares at him in wounded disbelief. She would marry this man. She would've married this man if he'd asked her any other way. She has never been married and hasn't regretted it. She wants to marry him, but all she can say is, "I'm not getting married so we can stay at a shelter!"

It never occurs to her that he is trying to hold on to her the only way he can.

❊ ❊ ❊

She grips the black plastic jail phone in one hand, holds the metal wrapped cord with the other. She feels like everything is slipping away. She is facing a lot of time. She's trying to get into a program, Drug Court or Mental Health Court, but they frown on violent crimes. Hard to get into a program with a violent crime. No matter how many diagnoses you have or how many days you were blacked out on drugs.

A program is her only chance of getting out of here, getting back to him. Not losing the only thing left that matters.

She talks to the receiver like it is him standing there. "Do you remember when you asked me to marry you and I said no?" Her wistful voice is heavy with the tears that slide unheeded, dripping splatter patterns on her orange smock top.

"I remember," he tells her.

His deep voice is both a comfort and a torture to her. All she wants. All she is going to lose.

"If I can get out," she says, "If I can get in a program and get out of here, would you still want to marry me?" She asks pinning all of her hope on his answer.

"I'll still marry you, girl," he says.

She believes him. She knows he means it. She leans her head against the cold steel phone wishing it was his chest. Relief warring with despair.

She wants it so badly, but she knows in her heart, she is probably not getting out. "I love you so much," she whispers, wishing for another chance.

She is trying to hold on. She is trying to build a lifeboat, a raft, anything to cling to in the midst of this tidal wave of consequences. She knows it will not save them. All of her life, she has tried to hold things together. Always, she has failed. She has no center and everything just keeps falling apart.

30. Healing (1) *2013*

The Faith and Character program isn't quite a joke. It could be, but she is determined to put something into it. To get something out of it. Whether any of the other 90 or so participants do or not.

She does not like the version of herself that caused her incarceration. If she cannot be someone else, then she sees no point in continuing on with this existence. Promise or no promise, Plan B is what Plan B has always been. Self-chosen euthanasia.

There has to be something besides this internal misery. She has to find a way out of or through it. If she can't or if she discovers there is nothing on the other side except more of the same, then Plan B will suffice. She cannot, simply will not, spend the next fourteen years in abject misery. She's had a lifetime of that already.

Sobriety is a beginning, but it is not enough. She is sober, but still miserable. She was miserable in the world, and this is so, so, much worse than the world. This place is awash in misery. The physical environment is miserable all on its own. Lack and hardship. She is well-acquainted with both. She can endure these, she has most of her life.

But the people. The constant barrage of other people's misery, rage, insanity, hopelessness, and all that stems from it. This is too much. It's too much to ask of one human being to endure the emotional and psychological detritus of a thousand others with no reprieve, no sanctuary, no refuge, or insulation.

She can barely function under the weight of her own brokenness.

She is looking for something. There has to be a beginning place, a starting point for change. Real change. Not just pretending. Saying the right words. Fake it til you make it rhetoric. She faked it until she wasn't able to fake it anymore. It didn't help her make it. It just helped disguise the reality of how bad things were. Attending 12-Step meetings in between binges. It was no good.

There has to be an authentic place to begin to change. She has to figure it out. A real first step. Even a tiny baby step. Just one thing that means something.

She committed to the program. She knows consistency is a foundation for change, the ground floor that everything else hinges upon. Ever since she lost her kids, she has had no consistency in her life. No reason to get up. No reason to work. No reason to care about anything. So she is starting with this, a commitment to consistency.

She discovers something else. Everyone around her is profoundly ungrateful. It is a cacophony of complaints from the time she wakes up, until she goes to sleep at night. From the person who has the most to the person who has the least. They all complain the same. They complain about what they have. They complain about what they don't have. They complain about what other people are doing or not doing. They complain relentlessly about the staff, the system, the state. It's all they do. Complain.

She can't find her way out of this misery, complaining with them. It only makes it worse.

She looks at the sunset.

She thinks about her children, how she would hold them when they were so small. The way their tiny arms would encircle her neck, so fragile. They felt like tiny sticks. The way they would lay against her like they were still a part of her flesh.

She is rusty at saying thank you. She hasn't talked with God, to God, or even at God in a long, long time.

She has been angry and pretends He isn't there. She's hurt and ignores Him. It hasn't been hard, really. It's like ignoring the sky or the sun. It's still there. You just stop seeing it.

But unlike the sky or the sun, inside she is afraid if she ignores Him long enough, He might go away and leave her truly alone.

Outside her housing unit is a rosebush. She sees it every day. She walks by it whenever she goes out or comes into the building. She watches women pick the flowers to make homemade potpourri. She picks up a fallen bloom. Her fingers caress the vibrant red petals. Softer than velvet. Softer than anything she's felt in years, now. It is the only spot of color in a grey and brown landscape.

"Thank you," she whispers. "Thank you for beauty."

"Thank you for all the love I have ever known," she adds thinking of her children.

It is what she can manage sincerely.

It is the first grain of gratitude she has been able to uncover on this seemingly endless beach of misery.

She doesn't know if it will be enough.

But it's a start.

31. Healing (2) *2013*

She is seated, along with ninety others, in plastic chairs arranged in a giant circle.

She watches with the others as this exercise unfolds. It is called The Wagon Wheel.

The character trait they are learning about is responsibility. In the Faith and Character Program, this translates to some combination of making amends and accountability.

A lot of people are choosing not to participate. She doesn't want to either, but she knows she will.

All year long, she has forced herself to do things that she had no desire to do. Stand up each day in class and say something. Something real. Share something brave and honest. It was very hard for her. She has never liked to be the center of attention. At least not when she was sober, and in here, you draw negative attention to yourself by having any integrity whatsoever. Her peers, for the most part, do not admire honesty, sobriety, or change. She has refused to let that deter her. She never cared what society thought of her when she lived in it, determined to destroy herself. She damn well won't let herself care what the people around her now think while she's trying to save herself.

This is a subculture of spoken and unspoken intimidation. They don't get her, but her refusal to bow under their judgment and her complete lack of concern for their opinions has won her a grudging sort of respect. She is brave, and they can't see her fear.

She watches as a woman stands in the center of the circle. Ninety-odd people stare along with her.

The woman has chosen 2. Two people to apologize to, the victim of her crime and her mother who is sick with cancer and now has no one to help take care of her.

There are many tears and much self-reproach. When she is finished, they all return to their seats in the circle leaving the center of the ring silent except for the clanging dread of whoever will be next.

She is chosen to be next. She asks for four people and the program director chooses them.

Four of her peers seat themselves in the center of the circle and she assigns them their identities. The first one is the victim of her crime, then her daughter, and two youngest sons.

Taking responsibility for her crime and apologizing to her victim isn't hard. It isn't personal. She was in the midst of a four-day drug-induced blackout when she committed her crime, and although she knows she committed it, she doesn't in fact remember much about it.

She does know that she had no right to inflict fear or harm upon another person and her remorse and apology are sincere. She may have spent her entire life hurting herself, but she never meant for it to hurt anyone else.

Then she speaks to her children. One by one. This is the hard part. This is the hardest part. To stand in front of all these strangers and bare her failure as a mother. She abhors displaying her grief and shame. She hates to cry in front of anyone, let alone a hard-eyed, critical crowd of convicts just like herself.

As she takes a deep breath, she tells herself, she isn't doing this for them.

She begins and the world narrows down to this moment. This circle of space. She doesn't even see the faces of her peers as she pours out her brokenness. She sees her daughter. Her son. Her autistic baby. She apologizes for abandoning them to the system. For letting their father take them. For not being stronger. She sobs as she tells them she is sorry for all the confusion and hurt that have made up their short lives. And she is sorry she'll never have a chance to do better. To be a better mother. She is sorry she was unable to put them first over her own pain and disappointments.

She is sorry she could not fix herself. That she failed them and that now it is too late. Most of all, she is sorry for all the pain still in front of them in a state system that will hold them hostage until they are 18. She cries every true thing she has never been able to say.

She is hollowed out. Empty. Emotionally devastated. The next day she cannot even leave her cell. She weeps continually and for no reason. She cannot stop.

It is as if a great and terrible wound has been ripped wide open and scraped out clean. All her edges are raw.

She takes out a notebook she has been haphazardly journaling in. She opens it and the words pour out like tears upon the paper.

For My Children

Who am I to ask forgiveness?
What is my bottomless well of pain
Compared to the ocean of yours?

Compared to your hurts
Your sorrows
Mine are nothing.
My failures are your wounds.
My life was a crisis
For so many reasons
And none.

There you stand, the survivors
Of an unnatural disaster.
And I pray
You are stronger
Than I ever was.
That you walk all the right paths
That I never showed you.
That you become all I ever dreamed
Yet never taught you to be.
Know that I have loved you.
That I love you
Even if you understandably and
Rightfully hate me always.

I will love you still.
I can't take back
All the books we didn't read

All the laughs we couldn't laugh together
All the tears that fell undried,
Unnoticed.

I wasn't there.
I am not there
To share your hurts
Your successes
Or your failures.

You are my success.
You survived my failure.

Sorry is such a small word
To symbolize a world of grief.

I only ask this:
That you shine like the sun.
Hold all your dreams
in the palm of your hand
and do not ever let them go.
Have enough love in your life,
in your heart, to overcome,
to heal the damage I have caused.

Be well. Be happy. Be loved.

Her grief has been a tsunami that crashed over her, obliterating everything in its path.

Driven onward by guilt and shame, the inevitable, engulfing wave kept an ensuing struggle desperate and roiling within her.

Now, looking down at those last two words, she feels something shift. Her pervasive sorrow begins to recede.

She feels like a survivor herself, awakening on a far distant shore.

And like a survivor, she starkly surveys the aftermath wondering what, if anything, can be rebuilt from this wreckage.

32. Dreams *2010*

She dreams she is flying with her middle son. He is laughing and she grabs him up, hugging him close in the sky. They spin, freewheeling aerialists.

She is at the old house where she grew up. She climbs up the steps, goes inside. There is strange music clattering from the radio on the counter.

Outside, through the window, she sees black clouds massing. The waterfield breaks with sudden pounding on the sheet iron roof. On the table, the car keys shine golden with their own light in the storm-shadowed gloom.

She goes out, the rain has turned to banks of snow. She sees a blanket edge protruding from an embankment. She pulls the edge, pulls it loose. Inside it unrolls a baby, blue with cold. Frozen. It is/is not hers.

She is standing in grass so green it looks otherworldly.

Her youngest son is on a swing. She walks toward him, grass springing deeply under her bare feet. He is sitting on the stilled swing, talking to her. She cannot quite hear what he is saying. She turns around, and he is gone. Empty swing swaying gently.

She heads into the trees, looking for him.

Passing through scenery where one snake eats another beneath a dogwood tree filled with webs of harm disguised by paper-masked caterpillars.

Stars shine weakly between glimpses of her daughter, a bright flash of blue, her youngest son's favorite shirt.

Her dog is running through the trees, helping her look for them, but she can never catch up.

She cannot find them.

She is walking through a landscape of bunk beds in rows. All painted white. There are women sitting on the metal bunks. They lead into the water. No one is talking. They do not see her, or each other.

Red backlit numbers flash reflecting the mirror's glass. Three forty-six a.m.

She lies awake holding on to the sound of her youngest son's voice. Her non-verbal, autistic son, who, in her dreams, has always spoken.

33. Period. *2015*

"The Department of Corrections has no interest in your rehabilitation," her one-time program facilitator had stated during her Faith and Character orientation. "You are here to be punished."

At no time during her incarceration has she heard a more honest statement from a D.O.C. employee. They do not care about her rehabilitation. So, she is rehabilitating herself.

She spent 3 years in the Faith and Character program. Her final year, she was a peer facilitator. She has met some amazing women in those three years. Women who should never have come to prison. Women who, despite injustice and personal tragedy, try to make their worst-case-scenario experiences into an opportunity for good.

Her friend who is about to leave is one of those women. She is from Mexico, but has lived in the United States for eight years prior to her incarceration. During her imprisonment, she taught herself to speak English fluently, was Character Champion of the Year their first year in the program together, and passed her G.E.D. while working full-time at the chapel.

Now she is going "home" to a country she hasn't seen in a dozen years, and she leaves in America her three children that the State of Oklahoma took and adopted out.

She will miss her friend dearly, but she will never forget the inspiration of her faith and strength.

She doesn't know how they manage it, these innocent women that the state maligns and slanders. Somehow they accept the monumental wrongs visited upon them by a system that so falsely touts justice. She has met many, surprisingly many, women here that have been falsely accused, railroaded, and wrongfully imprisoned. For accidents, for other people's actions (usually men), for the convenience of the state and for conviction records that benefit prosecutors and judges (padding their resumes). She wishes she could stop being utterly astonished by the depth of corruption, concealment, and collusion that judges, D.A.s, and public defenders operate in every day. She can't, though, because this is the new reality-laid-bare that she finds herself in. There is a seemingly endless parade of examples of the prevailing gender-biased injustice that defines this state, and like the prison she inhabits, there is no escaping it.

Once you're here, it is almost impossible to get out. Innocent or not. One woman just got released—exonerated by DNA evidence—after over 20 years of being wrongfully incarcerated. She was by far not the only one. They sentenced her to life in prison at 16 or 17 years old. She would've died in this prison, innocent of any crime, if not for the concentrated efforts of a (very) few people and the incontrovertible DNA evidence that ultimately set her free. Many others don't have that jackpot combination going for them.

And the state doesn't actually care if you're innocent or guilty. It's really better for them, if you are (by chance) innocent, to remain locked up with your "guilty" label. Then they never have to admit they were wrong—even if they knew it the whole time. Unfortunately, most people's attitudes only contribute to the problem and make it easier for the state to keep doing what they do best (which is locking up the poor). Because most people think that if you're in prison then you must deserve it, and if you have a 15, 20, 30 year sentence or a life sentence, then you must have done something unspeakable to deserve it, too. Period.

It doesn't really matter if the stories the prosecutors weave together are true or not. They don't have to be true. People just have to believe it. When the media loves to sensationalize any terrible story, fact or fiction, it just adds to the power of the state. That is all the help the justice system needs in a state where almost every felony carries a sentence of zero to life. No regulatory boards, no review of sentencing, not in the counties or over judges and D.A.s. No one is sentencing zero in Oklahoma. Twenty to life is pretty much the new average. This translates to life sentences and death sentences. Period.

34. Healing (3) *2016*

There is a new program that has been allowed to come in. It is called Poetic Justice and she is thrilled to be in one of the very first classes.

There are 2 classes starting simultaneously, so 50 women stand in front of the newly constructed brick chapel waiting.

No one knows what to expect. She sees a couple of people she knows from a previous writing class and some people she knows from the Faith and Character program. New programs are rare here. Usually they are shutting programs down, not bringing them in.

She watches the women surrounding her. She talks with some. Studiously avoids others. This is what it's like, she thinks, to have your life packed into a sardine can. Everything you want to do, there's 10 people you'd prefer to avoid already there in front of you. She's learned to let it go. To do the next thing she needs to do to be the person she wants to be. Regardless of who is watching, talking, laughing, judging. This small enclosed habitat is overwhelmed with people who would like to see you quit, want to discourage you. They like nothing better than to watch someone fail or give up, it makes you more like them.

She studies the sky, the clouds, tunes out the surround sound negativity. She watches the gate waiting for the new volunteers to appear. Curiously avid for a first look. So is everyone else.

They come through the gate. Several women in various stages and descriptions of life experience. Bright, friendly, talkative.

They all go inside, split up the classes, get on the count sheet.

In her class, they set up tables and everyone gets seated. The volunteers open up with how this program started at David L. Moss—which is Tulsa County Jail. She knows it well having spent 254 days there before transporting here.

They talk about writing as healing. Therapy. There is a breathing exercise. Relaxation/meditation technique they start the class with. She is familiar with exercises like this, though she can tell most of the women aren't.

She had done them before, as a kid in state's custody and also later by herself when she was trying to learn to control her thinking. Her racing thoughts. In for a 4-count, hold for 7, exhale for 8-count.

It seems a little surreal to be doing this now, in prison with a room full of strangers, but this is what her life looks like today. This moment. She tries to settle into it.

They'll read some poems, give a prompt, the volunteers continue to outline the class to them. Then they'll share out loud what they've written. She likes the disclaimer-free atmosphere, the tagline "get a load of this" instills.

They make their own rules. No judging. Respect the poet. She watches as a group of wary, skeptical inmates transform into a writing group, giving encouragement, finger-snapping applause. They're suddenly hipsters, beatniks, bohemians. She likes it.

They are going to write about a safe place. That is the prompt. The room goes still and quiet. An eerie miracle in prison. They only have fifteen minutes to write. Papers shifting quietly rustle. Pens and pencils begin scritching away. She stares at her paper. She thinks about when she was very small, maybe 4 or 5. When it was just her and her first baby brother. Once in a while they would sleep at her mother's mother's house. The furniture that seemed so nice. How her brother slept at one end of the couch and her, the other. How they played under the big sturdy table and in the hedge bushes outside. It was good there, but it wasn't real. That was just a bright shadow of hope.

She picks up her pen and writes the truth she knows, the one stamped into her bones: **No Safe Place** at the top of the page.

Her pen begins flying across the paper, line after line. She is no longer in the prison chapel classroom. She is 12. It is summer, and she is going to the river.

❖ ❖ ❖

There is no safe place, she writes. The only place I am safe is a place where I am alone. I am twelve, maybe, before state's custody or just after a brief stint at the Francis Willard Home for Girls. Which didn't last long because I ran away.

So, I am twelve and it's summer. I remember because I am wearing shorts and tennis shoes with no socks, but the shorts don't have front pockets, and I have a cigarette pack in my back pocket. Or maybe the shorts don't have pockets and the cigarette pack is in my shoe. And some matches. One cigarette—it's my last one and a paper book of matches. I am going down by the river.

The Poteau River runs red and muddy over the hill on the backside of my mom and dad's property. I go through the first set of woods and pass the pond where I used to go swimming with Thor before I went to the group home and my dad shot him for biting my youngest brother.

I go up the next hill and back into the trees which are mainly oak with full green leaves that rustle busily in the breeze. At the top of the hill, which stops abruptly, a much steeper, slicker, scarier descent downward begins. You have to watch out. The upside is all fallen leaves from a hundred years of autumns and rocks with pretty patches of moss the color of bleached verdigris, but the downside is slick, hard, bald mud and skinny trees with no helpful handholds.

There are sudden ditches and gullies that pepper the sliding, sidling, stuttering fast progress with half jumps and sudden full out leaps. Sweating and winded but feeling victorious to have made it to the bottom without having wiped out big time on the way down.

So here I am. And it's damp. The river is swift, muddy red brown with tiny eddies and whirlpools, and I wonder if it's full of leeches or if I'd drown if I jumped in and how I'd get back out. But I don't.

I find a place to sit. There are deer tracks deep in the steep muddy bank, and I see a tree growing sideways out of the ground. This is where I sit. The river makes a soft noise. I don't think you could hear it if you weren't alone, listening for it. The leaves and hanging vines flutter and creak. It's cooler here by the water. I am all sweat, bark, and the unnoticeable detritus of trees and dirt. I only smell the green, though. Fecund mud and water and all the things people grew out of. I am my own tribe. I am alone. I take out my tobacco offering to myself and the sharp sulfur of the match stings my nose as the bright burst of ignition stings my eyes. The acrid wildfire smoke stings my throat and lungs. It tastes like shit. It tastes like heaven.

I smoke and watch something rustling in the brush on the far bank. It is probably an armadillo. And I guess it doesn't know it should be afraid of people because you are only safe when you are alone.

He'll figure it out.

Prey always learns.

❊ ❊ ❊

They announce that the time is up and she lays her pen down. She is mildly stunned at how effortlessly all of that just poured out onto the paper. She's written off and on her whole life, but for the most part, poems. Not stuff like that. Not fragments of a life she stopped thinking about decades ago.

It is her turn to share and she reads without hesitation. She finishes the last line and looks up from the paper. She takes in the looks of mutual understanding that many of the faces in the room reflect.

Finger-snapping applause.

But the real applause, for her, lies in the resonating truths shared in this room.

There is healing here, she thinks, as the class ends.

35. Hope *2017*

They are having the Poetic Justice Graduation Party/Christmas Party. It is January, but no one cares. Spirits are high with good humor. There will be a little food, some gifts, and an open mic for poetry reading. She is excited about the open mic. She grabbed the best thing she thinks she's written so far and brought it with her just in case. Her whole life she's wanted to attend and participate in an open mic poetry reading. This is the closest she's ever got.

The food is Chick-Fil-A and salted caramel cupcakes. Quite a hit, especially for people who haven't had real world food in 5, 10, or 20 years.

Then is the gift giving, which turns out to be the 1st and 2nd editions of Poetic Justice Anthologies. The first edition is from David L. Moss, but the second edition has poetry from her class and she is surprised and delighted to see that her "No Safe Place" made it in. She hadn't expected it.

Finally, it's the open mic, and after the first couple of people, she goes up, clutching the paper in damp hands.

She is nervous, but determined.

She speaks into the microphone.

Close to Tangible

> Watching the moon grow
> like a fingernail until magically
> it turns into a coin
> then eats itself down to nothing.
>
> Trees shed hopeful dressings
> the grass withdraws from life
> birds flee through the air
>
> Holidays are just small words
> printed at the bottom of the boxes

on the calendar
—days the bed can go unmade
the refuge of sleep undenied.

Memories are mud
and you can get stuck in them
if you're not careful
which paths you take
which dreams you dream.

Everywhere the eye lights
on blue words and pictures
tattooed on face and body
telling their stories.

Mine are told in scars and the silences
I don't find uncomfortable or speak to fill.
I spill them on paper instead.

This is the part where I shape my words
into something close to tangible
It tastes like pills and smoke
It looks like frost glittering
on bars and fences. Strange patterns
revealed frozen on concrete
It sounds like a cricket lost in the vent
chirping night after day after night
It smells like burning copper wire,
fresh coffee brewing, sex on
dirty sheets, baked chicken and still-
warm spoons dark with residue

It feels like being too high
driving too fast

The wreck
The morning after

It would tell everything
and change nothing

There is loud and validating applause. She has a sense of satisfaction that she is not sure she has ever experienced before. But the best part of the night comes when they announce that they are expanding Poetic Justice to include an Advanced Class for those who have graduated. So they get to keep writing, sharing, connecting. She knows it is going to be amazing. She feels like there is a new story unfolding. A story of change and hope. She can't wait to be a part of it.

36. Made *2018*

Pounded flat

Folded, turned

Pounded flat

Folded, turned

Pounded flat

Pounded flat a thousand times.

This is how a sword is made

This is how a warrior is made

This is how a woman

is made

Phoenix awakens
Reborn to fly only to find
She must shine caged

Fin

CPSIA information can be obtained
at www.ICGtesting.com
Printed in the USA
LVHW082209011120
670397LV00011BA/1299